meeting JESUS

SUSAN F. TITUS

 STANDARD PUBLISHING

Cincinnati, Ohio   13-03374

Cover illustration by Corbin Hilliam
Inside illustrations by Dan Dunham

Library of Congress Cataloging-in-Publication Data

Titus, Susan F.
      Meeting Jesus: 26 junior high programs/by Susan F. Titus.

    1. Jesus Christ—Miricales. 2. Church group work with teenagers. I. Title.
BT366.T57   1990   232.9'55'0712—dc 20   90-32104
ISBN 0-87403-744-1   CIP

Scripture quotations are from The New International Version.
© 1973 by the New York Bible Society International,
used by permission.

© 1990, Susan F. Titus.
Published by The STANDARD PUBLISHING Company, Cincinnati, Ohio.
A division of STANDEX INTERNATIONAL Corporation.
Printed in U.S.A..

Contents

How Can We Meet Jesus?

Can you imagine meeting Jesus face to face? This book contains stories of individuals whose lives were changed forever after encountering Jesus.

John 17 presents Jesus' prayer for His disciples. This prayer was written for future Christians as well as for believers who lived during the time of Jesus. The prayer ends with these words:

'Righteous Father, though the world does not know you, I know you, and they know that you have sent me. I have made you known to them, and will continue to make you known in order that the love you have for me may be in them and that I myself may be in them'" (John 17:25, 26).

People, past and present, whom Jesus has touched are set apart for a unique task. The Greek word used in the New Testament for "set apart" not only means to be set apart for some special office or responsibility, but it also means to equip a person with the qualities of mind, heart, and character necessary for the task.

Meeting Jesus can be used in preparing young people to be who and what God desires them to be. Through studying the Scriptures and placing themselves in the shoes of personalities who actually met Jesus, young teens can follow the positive role models portrayed. Through the negative role models, junior highers can view some of their own weaknesses. The students can look at themselves, their emotions, and their problems through the lives and confrontations of these Biblical individuals.

The **Scripture** version suggested for use is the *New International Version*. Begin the sessions by having one or more students read the Scriptures aloud. If the passage is long, a different youth might read each paragraph. Every member of the class should use his own Bible to follow the reading of the lesson passage.

Teacher's Tidbits provides the youth leaders with interesting facts and Biblical background. This information should be studied prior to class, ideally the week before. Although this section is not read in class, it gives the leader a basis for discussing and answering the students' questions.

What to Bring indicates the supplies needed for the session.

Questions for Discussion lists questions that can help young teens understand the Biblical text and apply it to their lives. Following the reading of the Scripture, the leader asks the questions and waits for the students to answer. Many of the questions have more than one answer. Occasionally, questions may be too difficult for the young people, and the leader can give the answer. Extra time should be allowed for the discussion questions that are denoted by an asterisk (*). These (*) questions make the passage relevant to each pupil's own life.

Activities add excitement and reinforcement, drawing the young people closer to Christ. Each lesson contains two activities which furnish a change in pace after the discussion of the twenty questions.

Thoughts for the Day inspire the students to center their lives on Jesus throughout the week. These can be read or summarized by the leader after the activity period.

Memory Verse supplies the students with Scripture to learn each week. Perhaps the leader can distribute 3"-by-5" cards on which the young people write the verse. Encourage the students to keep the cards with them to memorize during the week. Some class time should be provided either at the beginning of the meeting or between activities for the students to say the previous week's memory verse. Recognition given for different levels of memory work completed is an excellent incentive.

Prayer concludes each lesson. The leader prays first and encourages the students to add prayers of their own. However, do not force students to pray out loud.

Next Week furnishes a preview of the upcoming week. It should be briefly mentioned after the prayer and before the class concludes.

A Biblical story, told to a young teen at the right moment, can make the truth crystal clear. Through this means, an interested adult might lead a youth to change his thoughts and actions. The stories and meanings of individual lives in the Bible can never be exhausted.

In the midst of today's frantic pace, young teens need to stop and listen to the voice of Jesus. His guidelines for behavior and actions are as applicable now as they were two thousand years ago. Perhaps these words can provide guidance for our young people today. This is the purpose of *Meeting Jesus*.

May everyone meet Jesus face-to-face in the lessons of this book.

Susan F. Titus
January 1990

John the Baptist Baptizes Jesus

Scripture Text

Matthew 3:1, 2, 11-17

Teacher's Tidbits

The leader should read this section at home before the day of the lesson.

When John the Baptist appeared as a flaming voice from God, the Jews were sadly conscious that no prophet had spoken for four hundred years. John fearlessly condemned evil wherever he found it, but his message was not merely a negative accusation. John's mission was to prepare people so they would recognize and accept Jesus when He appeared.

John the Baptist called the people to repent. Repentance is the turning away from sin and the turning toward God and the life He wants us to live. One outward sign of repentance is baptism. Repentance is absolutely essential.

The phenomenal success of John's ministry was evident in the thousands who came from all over southern Palestine to hear him.

In spite of his powerful influence, his attitude toward the promised Messiah showed humility. He hesitated to baptize God's Son because he felt unworthy of the task.

Before the time of John the Baptist, Jews never submitted to being baptized. They only used baptism for converts who came into Judaism from other religions. With the arrival of John the Baptist, they realized their own sin and need for God's forgiveness. However, Jesus was sinless and did not need a baptism of personal repentance. His baptism provided an opportunity for those He came to save to better identify with Him. By believing in Jesus Christ, we too can enter His kingdom and receive eternal life.

What to Bring

Bibles, pencils, paper, and a copy of the word search from page 7 for each student.

Questions for Discussion

There may be more than one correct answer for each of the following questions. The leader will ask the questions and wait for the students to provide the answers. The leader should not supply an answer unless it is necessary.

1. How do you picture John the Baptist in your mind? (*Wore a coarse, camel's hair tunic tied with a leather belt, shaggy beard, rugged features, tall, and strong.*)

2. What did John mean by the word "repent"? (*Change your mind, change your behavior, turn toward God.*)

*3. What does the word "repent" mean to you personally? Can you think of a time when you repented? (*Turning away from the things we are doing wrong, being sorry for our mistakes, turning toward God.*)

*4. What is the difference between saying "I'm sorry" and truly repenting? (*Repenting requires a change within ourselves that will show in our actions.*)

5. What did John mean by the words, "The kingdom of heaven is near"? (*God came to earth through His Son, Jesus Christ.*)

6. What types of people did John the Baptist address? (*The common people as well as Pharisees, Sadducees, publicans, and soldiers.*)

7. How successful was John's evangelizing? Why? (*He exerted a powerful influence. Thousands came from Jerusalem, all of Judea, and all over Palestine to hear his message.*)

*8. How can you borrow John's methods for getting friends to listen about Jesus and consider following

Him? (*Invite them over to your house or to a social activity at church, be open and friendly, just be yourself.*)

9. What personality traits did John show when he spoke about Jesus? (*Humility, reverence, awe. He did not feel qualified to carry Jesus' sandals.*)

*10. How can you be humble without being a doormat? (*Be unpretentious and modest, but not afraid to express your views.*)

*11. How should you respond to compliments? (*Say "thank you" but do not keep drawing attention to yourself.*)

*12. Have you experienced or watched a baptism? What were your feelings? (*Let several students share their experiences.*)

13. Why didn't Jesus need baptism? (*He was sinless.*)

14. Why did Jesus come to be baptized? (*So those He came to save could better identify with Him.*)

15. What did Jesus say to John? (*"It is proper for us to do this to fulfill all righteousness."*)

16. What did He mean by this? (*Through the death of Jesus on the cross, our wrongdoings are forgiven and we are considered worthy before God.*)

17. How did John experience the Spirit of God? (*The Spirit descended like a dove and rested on Jesus.*)

18. What did the voice from heaven say? (*"This is my Son, whom I love; with him I am well pleased."*)

*19. How can you be God's spokesperson without appearing strange when you are around people who have never heard about Jesus? (*Tell them why your life is better because He is part of it. Be careful not to use Christian words that they may not understand.*)

*20. Challenge: Tell one of your friends, neighbors, or family members about Jesus Christ as John the Baptist did.

Activity 1: Introduce a Friend

This activity is appropriate for the beginning of the session. It will help everyone become better acquainted and feel more relaxed in the group discussion.

Have the students form a circle and number off "one," "two," "one," "two," and so on around the circle. Each "one" becomes a partner with the "two" on his left. Ask the following questions and allow five minutes for partners to exchange information about themselves.

1. What is the most interesting thing you have done?

2. Where is the most exciting place you have been? When time is up, have each student introduce his partner to the others in the circle by telling his name and answering the questions.

Activity 2: Word Search

John the Baptist told about the coming of Jesus. Ask the students to find the words hidden in the word search from page 7. Each student should have his own copy. (*Puzzle solution is located on page 8.*)

Thoughts for the Day

The leader should summarize the ideas presented in these thoughts.

Thousands came to be baptized by John the Baptist. John's purpose was to prepare the people so they would recognize and accept Jesus when He appeared.

John the Baptist was a person who met Jesus and baptized Him. Like John, we can tell others about Jesus. Then our friends and family members who never heard about God's Son can follow Him and have eternal life.

Memory Verse

A copy of the memory verse should be made for each student to take home. After the leader distributes the copies, the class can say the verse aloud together.

"'Repent, for the kingdom of heaven is near'" (Matthew 3:2).

Prayer

To conclude the session, the leader leads in prayer, allowing time for individual prayers by the students.

Dear God, forgive us for the things we do wrong. Help our actions to be pleasing to You. Thank You that we can learn about John the Baptist. Teach us to help others to know Your Son. In Jesus' name, amen.

Next Week

The leader briefly mentions the next week's lesson, "The Devil Tempts Jesus in the Desert" (Matthew 4:1-11). What happened during the forty days Jesus spent alone in the desert? What did Satan hope to achieve by tempting Jesus? Next week we will study the personal confrontation between Jesus Christ and Satan.

John the Baptist

Matthew 3:1, 2, 11-17

Words

BAPTIZE
REPENTANCE
SANDALS
HOLY SPIRIT
RIGHTEOUSNESS

HEAVEN
FULFILL
JORDAN
DOVE
JOHN THE BAPTIST

```
D  O  W  E  J  O  H  N  T  H  E  B  A  P  T  I  S  T  D  O  D
R  D  O  S  L  P  H  A  P  O  O  H  U  F  T  D  L  H  B  Z  V
E  U  H  H  P  G  D  D  I  L  O  G  T  D  G  F  A  O  G  S  S
P  K  I  E  O  H  R  R  Y  Y  F  U  R  S  F  W  D  O  U  S  P
E  G  H  A  O  G  I  O  O  S  T  L  O  I  T  D  N  O  T  E  S
N  O  U  V  E  T  R  J  L  P  L  R  U  F  C  S  A  H  V  P  A
T  I  O  E  O  T  R  I  D  I  O  U  E  W  S  L  S  S  D  E  D
A  U  O  N  H  J  F  S  F  R  P  U  H  O  U  Y  L  O  A  U  E
N  O  H  N  I  L  O  L  R  I  G  H  T  E  O  U  S  N  E  S  S
C  T  Y  E  U  R  U  G  H  T  S  T  E  I  N  E  S  S  E  D  F
E  Y  H  F  U  F  T  B  A  P  T  I  Z  E  R  G  I  O  A  S  T
```

Solution

```
              J O H N T H E B A P T I S T
R             A     O                     L
E       H     D     L                     A
P       E     R     Y                     D
E       A     O     S     L               N O
N       V     J     P L                   A V
T       E           I                     S     E
A       N        F  R
N              L R I G H T E O U S N E S S
C             U     T
E          F  B A P T I Z E
```

The Devil Tempts Jesus in the Desert

Scripture Text

Matthew 4:1-11

Teacher's Tidbits

On the central plain of Palestine, a wilderness stretches from Jerusalem to the Dead Sea. The hills are covered with yellow sand, and jagged rocks jut out from the blistered limestone. Little vegetation grows in this desolation. The ground shimmers like a huge furnace from the heat.

In that wilderness, Jesus could be more alone than anywhere else in Palestine. He fasted there for forty days soon after His baptism. He was tested there by Satan.

This lesson recounts one of the most mysterious battles of all time—the personal confrontation between Jesus Christ and Satan. Even during extreme temptation, Jesus consistently lived in perfect harmony with God's divine plan. He demonstrated His full commitment to His Father. He confirmed His power over hell and His victory over sin.

Satan did not doubt that Jesus was the Son of God. He wanted Jesus to demonstrate His deity through a miraculous work to gain worldly recognition and satisfy those who were doubting. Satan wanted Jesus to compromise His values and serve him.

We, too, are tested to see whether we will use spiritual privileges to glorify God or for our own self-interests.

What to Bring

Bibles, pencils, paper, and four copies of the skit from Activity 1.

Questions for Discussion

There may be more than one correct answer for each of the following questions. The leader will ask the questions and wait for the students to provide the answers. The leader should not supply an answer unless it is necessary.

1. How do you picture the Palestine wilderness in your mind? (*Jagged rocks jutting out of blistered limestone, hills covered with yellow sand, sparse vegetation, overpowering dry heat.*)

*2. Have you spent time walking in a desert? How did you feel physically and emotionally? (*Parched mouth, headache from the heat, loneliness.*)

*3. What does hunger do to a person's mental attitude? (*Weakens a person's moral and spiritual resistance; makes an individual grumpy.*)

*4. What does the word "tempt" mean to you? (*Test, entice, lure, tantalize.*)

5. What was the first temptation presented to Jesus by Satan? (*Satan told Him to tell the stones to become bread.*)

6. What do you think the devil was trying to accomplish by this temptation? (*He wanted Jesus to use His power for His own benefit, satisfying His hunger.*)

7. What was Jesus' answer? (*"Man does not live on bread alone, but on every word that comes from the mouth of God."*)

*8. When do you find it hardest to say no to things you should not do? (*When you are tired or hungry.*)

9. What was the second proposal presented by the devil? (*That Jesus throw Himself down from a pinnacle of the temple.*)

10. What was the purpose of this test? (*Satan wanted Jesus to demonstrate His deity through a miraculous work.*)

11. How did Jesus reply? (*"Do not put the Lord your God to the test."*)

*12. Why does Satan want you to give in to wrong thoughts or actions? (*It weakens your reputation and your relationship with Christ.*)

13. What was the final temptation? (*The devil asked Jesus to bow down and worship him.*)

14. What did Satan offer in return? (*Jesus could rule the world, could become King of kings without a cross and without a struggle.*)

*15. Is it all right for a believer to become popular, powerful, or rich? (*Yes, if you do not compromise your standards.*)

16. What did the devil hope to accomplish by this final temptation? (*He wanted Jesus to attain divine goals by worldly means.*)

17. How did Jesus respond? (*"Away from me, Satan. Worship the Lord your God and serve Him only."*)

*18. Is it wrong to be tempted? Explain. (*No, it is wrong to give in to temptation. Everyone is tempted.*)

*19. How can you be strong when facing temptation? (*Establish and understand your own moral code; say "no" when needed; choose quality friends.*)

*20. Challenge: Be aware of Satan's attacks. Say "no" to one thing that you know is wrong this coming week.

Activity 1: Lost-and-Found Drama

The only props necessary for this skit are a billfold stuffed with play money, a table, and a chair. Place the chair at the table. Select four students to participate. Make a copy of the following skit for each actor.

(*The scene opens with Jim and Hank walking along the beach.*)

Jim: Look over there in the sand.

Hank: I don't know, but I'll grab it before the tide carries it away. (*He runs forward a few steps, then bends down to pick up the billfold.*) Looks like a wallet.

Jim: Let's see if there is any identification in it.

Hank: (*Opens the wallet.*) Look at all the money. There must be over a hundred dollars here!

Jim: Hank, is there a driver's license?

Hank: There's enough money here to buy a surfboard, Jim.

Jim: But the money's not ours.

Hank: We've been saving all summer for that blue board in the surf shop window. (*Holds up a fist full of play money.*) Here's our surfboard, Jim.

Jim: How much money is there? (*The boys count the money.*)

Hank: One hundred and twenty-three dollars.

Jim: (*Softly.*) That is enough for a surfboard.

Hank: Surf shop, here we come!

Jim: Not so fast. Let me see that wallet. (*He takes the wallet from Hank.*) Here's a driver's license. It belongs to Patrick H. Long.

Hank: He must be loaded to carry around that much cash. I'm sure he won't miss a hundred or so.

Jim: No, Hank. I want that surfboard as much as you do, but I don't feel right taking some man's money. Let's turn it in at the police station.

(*The boys turn around. The police officer brings his chair onto the stage and sits behind the real or imaginary desk. The elderly man stands in front of him. Jim walks up to the police officer.*)

Jim: (*Handing the wallet to the police officer.*) Officer, we found this wallet on the beach this afternoon.

Elderly man: I sure hope it's mine, son. Went for a walk on the beach this morning. Lost my wallet.

Officer: (*Opens the wallet.*) You're in luck, Mr. Long. This is yours. (*He hands the wallet to the man.*)

Elderly man: (*Clutches the wallet.*) Thanks, boys. I just cashed my Social Security check. All the money I

have to live on for a month is in that wallet.

Jim: (*Glancing at Hank.*) We're happy to help, Mr. Long.

Activity 2: Making Words From Temptation

Give each student a piece of paper and a pencil. Have them write the word "temptation" at the top of the page. Ask them to see how many words of three letters or more can be made from temptation. Allow five minutes for them to write down their words. The person with the most words wins.

Thoughts for the Day

The leader should summarize the ideas presented in the following thoughts.

Shortly after His baptism, Jesus was tested by Satan in the Palestine wilderness. Jesus was encouraged to satisfy His hunger by using divine powers, to demonstrate His deity through a miracle, and to worship Satan. He resisted all temptations.

We too are approached by Satan. He checks to see if we are depending on God's strength or our own—to see if we are using our talents for God's glory or our own self-interests.

Memory Verse

A copy of the memory verse should be made for each student to take home. After the leader distributes the copies, the class can say the verse.

"'Man does not live on bread alone, but on every word that comes from the mouth of God'" (Matthew 4:4).

Prayer

To conclude the session, the leader leads in prayer, allowing time for individual prayers by the students.

Dear Lord, every day we are faced with decisions. Help us not to be tempted to do the things that we know are wrong. In Jesus' name, amen.

Next Week

The leader briefly mentions the next week's lesson, "Nathanael Responds to Jesus' Call" (John 1:43-51). Next week we will study about a little-known disciple named Nathanael.

Nathanael Responds to Jesus' Call

Scripture Text

John 1:43-51

Teacher's Tidbits

Nothing in the Old Testament foretold of Jesus coming from Nazareth. Nathanael was an honest skeptic who wondered if anything good could come out of the insignificant village of Nazareth. Nevertheless, he traveled with Philip to meet Jesus.

Questioning and doubting are not wrong. Skepticism is a legitimate starting point, but it cannot have the last word. Questioning often leads to a deeper understanding. But when facts are not provided, we need to step out in faith and accept what God is trying to tell us.

Nathanael's name means "the gift of God." He is never referred to in Matthew, Mark, or Luke. However, Bartholomew is a last name mentioned in the other three gospels, so many scholars think he and Nathanael are the same person.

Nathanael knew that Jesus could not have seen him under the fig tree. Whatever doubts had filled his mind vanished instantaneously when Jesus spoke to him. He called Jesus "Rabbi," which means teacher. He claimed Him as "the Messiah," hailing Jesus with the highest title the Judaic faith could bestow.

What to Bring

Bibles, pencils, paper, and a copy of the Bible verse in code from Activity 1 for each student.

Questions for Discussion

There may be more than one correct answer for each of the following questions. The leader will ask the questions and wait for the students to provide the answers. The leader should not supply an answer unless it is necessary.

1. What did Philip do when Jesus said, "'Follow me'"? (*He located Nathanael and told him about Jesus.*)

2. How did Philip describe Jesus? (*As the One Moses and the prophets wrote about, Jesus of Nazareth—the son of Joseph.*)

3. Do you know how a man was usually identified in Biblical times? (*The name of his father and his home town were added to a man's personal name.*)

4. How did Nathanael react? (*Can anything good come from Nazareth?*)

5. Why do you think he reacted this way? (*Nazareth was an insignificant, small town. He expected Jesus to come from a large, important city.*)

*6. Have you ever judged a person by how they dressed or where they were from? Explain. (*Allow time for several to share incidents when they misjudged people by their looks or jumped to conclusions because of gossip.*)

7. Did Philip try to argue with his friend? How did he react? (*No. He replied, "'Come and see.'"*)

*8. Have you argued with a friend when he disagreed with you? Explain. (*Allow time for several students to share their experiences.*)

*9. What would be a better way to react when someone opposes your view? (*Show him by example what you mean, but allow him to state and hold his own opinion. Arguments often do more harm than good.*)

*10. Is it all right to question and doubt? (*Yes, often questioning leads to a better understanding.*)

11. Why did Jesus tell Nathanael that He saw him under the fig tree? (*Jesus wanted Nathanael to realize that He knew everything about him.*)

12. How did Nathanael react to Jesus' description of him? (*He declared, "'Rabbi, you are the Son of God; you are the King of Israel.'"*)

13. Why was Nathanael's reaction surprising? (*Before meeting Jesus he acted skeptical. Also, Jesus had not revealed who He was yet, so Nathanael's answer was surprising.*)

14. What do you remember about the story of Jacob at Bethel? (*The angels of God were going up and down the ladder to Heaven.*)

15. Why do you think Jesus called Himself the Son of Man? (*He wanted people to know that He understood them.*)

*16. What does this mean to you personally? (*Allow time for several students to answer. Jesus under-*

stands us, too. He knows where we live and what we do.)

17. What else did Jesus refer to in this verse? (*His crucifixion.*)

*18. What are some of the things that Jesus knows about you? (*He knows your name, where you live, everything you do. Nothing is hidden from His eyes.*)

*19. How can Jesus help you because of His knowledge of you? (*He knows the solutions to all our problems; He knows what will happen before it occurs; He loves us and wants to help us.*)

*20. Challenge: Ask Jesus to help you solve one problem this coming week.

Activity 1: Decode the Secret Message

Every student should have a piece of paper with the secret message and the code on it. Allow ten minutes for the class to decode the secret message.

a=! c=@ d=# e=$ f=% g=^ h=& i=* k=(l=) m=-
n=+ o=[p=] r=" s=' t=< u=> v=? w=/ y=x

[ )["#, x[> &!?$ '$!"@&$# -$!+# x[> (+[/ -$.

x[> (+[/ /&$+ * '*< !+# /&$+ * "*'$:

x[>]$"@$*?$ -x <&[>^&<' %"[- !%!".

Solution

O Lord, you have searched me and you know me.
You know when I sit and when I rise:
You perceive my thoughts from afar.

Activity 2: Numbering the Disciples

Have the students form a circle with their chairs. Ask them to number off starting with one and going clockwise around the circle. Each person will have his own number.

Have the students start by slapping their hands on their knees twice, clapping their hands twice, and snapping their fingers on each hand alternately. On the first snap, player 1 says his own number. On the second snap, he says the number of another player. (*For example: 1—6.*)

Then player 6 slaps his knees, his hands, and snaps his fingers twice calling out 6—3. Then it is Player 3's turn. Continue in this manner with everyone following the rhythm of the person whose number was called. If someone does not hear his number or breaks the rhythm, he must go to the end of the circle and take the largest number as his own. Everyone else moves up one chair and one number. (*For exam-*

ple: Player 6 becomes Player 5.*) The game may be continued as long as time permits.

Thoughts for the Day

The leader should summarize the ideas presented in the following thoughts.

Philip wanted to share the news when he discovered who Jesus was, so he told his friend Nathanael. This is how the number of Christians increases today, with one person telling the Good News to another.

Jesus read the thoughts of Nathanael's innermost heart. Nothing is hidden from His eyes. He also knows our past and our desires.

Memory Verse

A copy of the memory verse should be made for each student to take home. After the leader distributes the copies, the class can say the verse aloud together.

"'O Lord, you have searched me and you know me.
You know when I sit and when I rise;
You perceive my thoughts from afar'" (Psalm 139:1, 2).

Prayer

To conclude the session, the leader leads in prayer, allowing time for individual prayers by the students.

Dear Lord, You know each of us by name. You know everything about us. Help us to overcome our doubts. Guide us as we share the Good News of You with our friends and family. In Jesus' name, amen.

Next Week

The leader briefly mentions the next week's lesson, "Nicodemus Hears About a Special New Birth" (John 3:1-21). Who was this Pharisee named Nicodemus? Next week we will study about a special new birth offered to Nicodemus and to all who believe.

Nicodemus Hears About a Special New Birth

Scripture Text

John 3:1-21

Teacher's Tidbits

The heart of Nicodemus was filled with an unsatisfied longing. Yet because he was a leading Pharisee and a member of the Sanhedrin, Nicodemus came cautiously to Jesus at night. He addressed Jesus as a fellow theologian, but he did not know Jesus as the Son of God. Nicodemus did not possess eternal life at this point even though he said complimentary things about Jesus.

Jesus' presence on earth created a double movement—those who came to Him to receive a blessing and those who withdrew from Him to hide and plot His destruction.

When a person is confronted with Jesus but does not accept Him as the Son of God, his own action condemns him. God sent Jesus in love. It is not God who condemns the person but the individual who convicts him#t is not God who condemns the person but the individual who convicts himself by not believing.

Jesus' answers to Nicodemus concerning rebirth were not new to Jews. When a person from another faith accepted Judaism by prayer, sacrifice, and baptism, he was regarded as being reborn. Jesus wanted Nicodemus to think for himself and to believe in Him.

Nicodemus came alone—he came directly to Christ. We, too, must do the same to be saved. Later, when the Jewish leaders planned to kill Jesus, Nicodemus timidly spoke up in the Sanhedrin and suggested the injustice of condemning a man without a trial. Then after the death of Jesus, Nicodemus came boldly with Joseph of Arimathea and assisted in the burial of the body of Jesus Christ. These events show how his faith grew.

What to Bring

Bibles, pencils, paper, and a copy of the unfinished story from Activity 1 for each student.

Questions for Discussion

There may be more than one correct answer for each of the following questions. The leader will ask the questions and wait for the students to provide the answers. The leader should not supply an answer unless it is necessary.

1. Who was Nicodemus? (*A leading Pharisee; a member of the Sanhedrin; a member of the Jewish ruling council.*)

2. Why do you think he came to Jesus at night? (*He was afraid his important public position might be lost if he was seen with Jesus.*)

3. Who did Nicodemus think Jesus was? (*A teacher from God who performed miracles.*)

4. Was Jesus pleased that Nicodemus admired Him? How did Jesus react? (*No, He wanted Nicodemus to recognize Him as the Son of God; He wanted Nicodemus to be saved.*)

*5. What words would you use to describe who Jesus is? (*Son of God; Savior of the world; Son of Man.*)

6. What do the water and the Spirit represent? (*Water stands for cleansing, and the Holy Spirit is the strengthening power of Jesus Christ.*)

7. What does it mean to be born of water and the Spirit? (*When Jesus comes into our lives, His strengthening power enables us to do things we never could do before.*)

8. How would you compare the Spirit and the wind? (*You may not understand how the wind blows, but you can see the results. You may not know how the Spirit works, but you can see the results in people's lives.*)

*9. Can you think of someone whose life was changed drastically when he learned about Jesus and was born again? (*Allow time for several students to share their experiences.*)

10. Why did God send Jesus into the world to be persecuted and die on the cross? (*Because God loves the world, and He wants all who believe to have eternal life. Jesus became a sacrifice for our sins.*)

11. Was Nicodemus a religious person? Describe his good qualities. (*Yes, he was an important Pharisee who taught the Word of God. He was moral, cultured, and seeking the truth.*)

12. Where did Nicodemus fall short? (*His faith was shallow; he admired Jesus but did not worship Him. He complimented Jesus, but he did not believe in Him and did not obtain eternal life at this point.*)

13. What are some other reasons that people of shallow faith were attracted to Jesus? (*He performed miracles; they considered Him a great teacher; He healed them; He fed them.*)

14. What were some of the actions of the people who withdrew from Jesus into the darkness? (*They hid to plot His destruction resulting in His crucifixion on the cross.*)

*15. How does darkness hide evil deeds today? (*Cars and houses are broken into; people are attacked and robbed usually at night. The attackers do not want to be seen or identified.*)

*16. Can you think of a time when you did something wrong and then hid the truth? (*Do not force anyone who is hesitant to speak on this personal question, but encourage everyone to silently recall such an incident.*)

*17. When a person is told about Jesus but does not accept Him, does Jesus condemn that individual? (*No, the person condemns himself with his own actions.*)

18. Did Nicodemus put Jesus first in his life? (*No, he placed himself first in importance.*)

*19. What are some things you can do to place Jesus first in your life? (*Pray about His will for the big and little concerns in life, think of other people's feelings, read and follow the Bible.*)

*20. Challenge: Make sure you place Jesus first in one important happening this next week.

Activity 1: What Would You Do?

Give a copy of the following, unfinished story to each student. Divide the class into groups of three or four. Allow ten to fifteen minutes for each group to read and finish the story. Then reconvene the class and have a leader from each group read their ending. Allow time for discussion.

Sam stepped outside the entrance to the library and looked up at the blackened sky. He wanted to get home before dark, but he was not going to make it. He zipped his windbreaker tightly around his neck and hurried down the sidewalk towards the park.

When he neared the entrance, he saw two shadows moving behind an old, oak tree. Then he heard ear-piercing screams. His heart pounded. What should he do?

Activity 2: Your qualities: Good and Bad

Give each student a piece of paper and a pencil.

Ask them to list their good qualities in a column on the left side of the paper. Then have the students list characteristics that they feel could be improved on the right side. Assure them that their answers are strictly between themselves and God. The lists will not be turned in, nor will they be read in class. Ask the students to take their lists home and pray about them.

Thoughts for the Day

The leader should summarize the ideas presented in the following thoughts.

Nicodemus felt an unsatisfied longing in his heart. He came to Jesus even though he feared being seen. Jesus confronted Nicodemus, but the choice was left up to the Jewish leader as to whether or not he would accept Christ as his Savior and as the Son of God.

Our Heavenly Father sent Jesus into the world to die for us because He loves us so much. He wants us to ask Jesus to enter our lives so that we can be all that He wants us to be through the strengthening power of the Holy Spirit. But, like Nicodemus, the choice is ours.

Memory Verse

A copy of the memory verse should be made for each student to take home. After the leader distributes the copies, the class can say the verse aloud together.

"'For God so loved the world that he gave his one and only Son, that whoever believes in him shall not perish but have eternal life'" (John 3:16).

Prayer

To conclude the session, the leader leads in prayer, allowing time for individual prayers by the students.

Dear God, thank You for sending Jesus into the world to die so that we can live eternally with You. Teach us to place You first in our lives. Help our actions to be pleasing to You. In Jesus' name, amen.

Next Week

The leader briefly mentions the next week's lesson, "The Samaritan Woman Meets Jesus at the Well" (John 4:4-26, 39-42). What happened to change the life of the Samaritan woman? Next week we will study about a special gift of living water offered by Jesus.

The Samaritan Woman Meets Jesus at the Well

Scripture Text

John 4:4-26, 39-42

Teacher's Tidbits

In 720 B.C. the Assyrians invaded and conquered the northern kingdom of Samaria. Many people were transported to Media, but those remaining intermarried with foreigners who worshipped many gods.

The result was the mongrel race of Samaritans who practiced a religion that was partly Jewish and partly heathen. The Samaritans accepted the Pentateuch, the first five books of the Old Testament, but they ignored the rest. They tampered with Scripture to glorify Mount Gerizem while totally rejecting Jerusalem.

The shortest distance from Judea in the south to Galilee in the north was through Samaria. However, the Jews despised the Samaritans and usually traveled the long way around to avoid contact with them. The journey through Samaria took three days; the alternate route took twice as long.

The strict rabbis did not allow men to greet women in public. However, Jesus was not controlled by religious and racial barriers.

When the woman was offered living water, she assumed Jesus meant running stream water as contrasted with the standing water of a well. But Jesus was speaking of salvation. He compelled the Samaritan woman to face herself, her immorality, and the inadequacy of her life.

What to Bring

Bibles, pencils, paper, the association words from Activity 2 written on 3"-by-5" cards, and a copy of the story with the missing words from Activity 1 for each student.

Questions for Discussion

There may be more than one correct answer for each of the following questions. The leader will ask the questions and wait for the students to provide the answers. The leader should not supply an answer unless it is necessary.

1. Who were the Samaritans? (*Jews who had intermarried with people who worshipped many gods. Their religion distorted scripture.*)

2. How did the Jews usually treat the Samaritans? (*They despised and avoided them.*)

3. Why is it surprising that Jesus spoke to the Samaritan woman? (*Men did not speak to women in public, and Jews never spoke to Samaritans.*)

*4. Can you think of an example when you have seen racial or sexual discrimination? (*Allow time for several students to cite examples.*)

*5. Have you experienced this type of discrimination in your own life? (*Do not force anyone who is not willing to share on this sensitive topic.*)

*6. Do you think people should be banned from certain jobs because of their sex? Explain. (*No, not if they are capable of doing the work.*)

7. How did the Samaritan woman react to Jesus? (*She was surprised that He asked her for a drink.*)

8. What did she think Jesus meant by "living water"? (*Running stream water.*)

9. Why do you think Jesus asked the woman to call her husband? (*He knew she did not have a husband, and He wanted to see if she would admit it to Him.*)

10. How did Jesus answer the question of whether it is better to worship on the mountain or in Jerusalem? (*God is not confined to things or places. It is not the place someone worships that counts but the attitude within one's own heart.*)

11. What does it mean to worship the Father in spirit and in truth? (*The most important part of each of us is our spirit displayed in the attitude of our hearts. True worship is when we focus our attention on God.*)

12. What is our spirit? (*The part within us that lasts when our earthly body is dead and buried. It is our innermost being which controls our attitudes.*)

13. Who did Jesus admit He was? (*The Messiah.*)

14. What caused other Samaritans to believe? (*The woman's testimony and the words of Jesus.*)

15. Why do you think the pagan Samaritan woman was open to Jesus while the Jewish leaders rejected Him? (*She realized that the life she was leading was wrong, and she was willing to trust Jesus and to change. But the Pharisees were self-righteous; they*

felt that they already had all the answers.)

16. Compare the Samaritan woman to Nicodemus? (*He came hesitantly and secretly to Jesus at night. The woman came boldly in daylight to Him. Then she invited her town to come and meet Him.*)

*** 17.** Have you boldly spoken about Jesus in front of others? Explain. (*Allow time for several students to talk about their experiences.*)

*** 18.** What are some stumbling blocks that you might encounter in speaking out? (*Some may reject what you are saying.*)

*** 19.** What is the reward for telling others about Jesus? (*Perhaps someone can meet Jesus through you and find the living water of salvation.*)

*** 20.** Challenge: This week, be a friend to an individual similar to the Samaritan woman who people dislike and avoid.

Activity 1: Fill in the Ten Missing Words

Give a copy of the following story with the missing words to each student. Allow ten minutes for the class, working individually, to fill in the blanks. Then have them take turns, each reading a sentence, to tell the whole story.

Jesus was tired from the journey so he sat by a _____.

A _____ woman came to draw water. Jesus said, "Will you give me a _____?" Jesus offered her the gift of _____ _____. He said that a time is coming when true worshippers will worship the Father in _____ and in _____. The woman said, "I know that _____ is coming. When He comes, He will explain _____ to us." Jesus answered, "I who speak to you am _____."

Solution

1. Well	**4.** Living Water	**7.** Messiah
2. Samaritan	**5.** Spirit	**8.** Everything
3. Drink	**6.** Truth	**9.** He

Activity 2: What Do You Associate With This Word?

Before class, the leader should print six 3"-by-5" cards with one word and number per card. The numbers represent the order in which the words will be used in the game.

1. Water	**3.** Spirit	**5.** Believe
2. Spring	**4.** Truth	**6.** Messiah

The class sits in a circle for this activity. If there are more than twenty students, form several circles. A set of three-by-five cards are needed for each circle.

Hand out the six cards to various students. The student who has "1. Water" printed on his card starts the game by saying the word.

The person to his left says the first word that he associates with water, such as "thirst." The person to his left says the word he associates with thirst. The game continues around the circle until everyone has a turn.

Then the person with the second word on his card says, "Spring." The person to his left responds, and the game continues until all six words are associated with other words around the circle.

Thoughts for the Day

The leader should summarize the ideas presented in the following thoughts.

Jesus spoke to the Samaritan woman even though it was not the Jewish custom to talk to women in public or to the despised Samaritans. In return, the woman trusted Jesus even though she did not fully understand who He was. She told the people of her town about Him. Many believed and truly realized that Jesus is the Savior of the world.

Where can we find God? Where can we worship Him? It is not the place where we worship God that counts but the attitude of our hearts. God, and His gift of living water, can be found anywhere.

Memory Verse

A copy of the memory verse should be made for each student to take home. After the leader distributes the copies, the class can say the verse.

"'But whoever drinks the water I give him will never thirst. Indeed, the water I give him will become in him a spring of water welling up to eternal life'" (John 4:14).

Prayer

To conclude the session, the leader leads in prayer.

Dear Lord, thank You for Your gift of living water. Help us not to discriminate against others. In Jesus' name, amen.

Next Week

The leader briefly mentions the next week's lesson, "An Official's Sick Son Becomes Healthy" (John 4:46-54). What happened when the royal official begged Jesus to come to his house? Next week we will study about the second miracle performed by Jesus at Cana.

An Official's Sick Son Becomes Healthy

Scripture Text

John 4:46-54

Teacher's Tidbits

The leader should read this section at home before the day of the lesson.

When news of Jesus' wonderful signs in Jerusalem spread through Galilee by the pilgrims returning from the recent Passover, the royal official listened. Although he held a high position at the court of Herod, he traveled twenty miles to beg a favor of the former, village carpenter.

Jesus rebuked the nobleman to test his faith. The official did not defend himself or argue. He simply urged Jesus to come with him before his son died.

Our Lord did not travel to the sickbed to be acknowledged as healer. Nor was a bargain made with the official to advertise the event if He cured the son. From twenty miles away, Christ quietly healed the young man.

The shallow faith of the nobleman became a genuine faith in Christ as Lord. He started home with nothing but the assurance of Jesus for comfort. Upon meeting his servants, he learned that the word of Jesus was indeed the word of authority. We, too, show our faith by believing what Jesus says is true.

The idea of Jesus as the Anointed One of God must have contradicted all of the man's preconceived notions. And it would be difficult for the official to profess his faith at the court of Herod. Yet, he and all his household believed—the first established case in the New Testament of an entire household believing.

In John's gospel, our Lord's miracles were signs to show who He is. Signs and wonders accompanied His ministry for that purpose exclusively. Yet, it is a mistake to assume because Jesus healed in this particular case that He cures every time. He did not heal Paul in the New Testament, nor did He restore Joni Eareckson Tada, a quadriplegic painter and author. A disabled body does not prevent Christian service.

What to Bring

Bibles, pencils, paper, and a copy for each small group of the discussion questions from Activity 2.

Questions for Discussion

There may be more than one correct answer for each of the following questions. The leader will ask the questions and wait for the students to provide the answers. The leader should not supply an answer unless it is necessary.

1. Where did Jesus visit? (*Cana in Galilee.*)
2. Why was it surprising that a royal official came to Jesus? (*He was a nobleman at Herod's court. Jesus' profession had been carpentry.*)
3. How do you think his friends and business associates would react if they knew where he sought help? (*They would probably laugh and mock him.*)
*4. Can you think of an example when you suffered from peer pressure because of something similar that you did? (*Allow time for several students to cite examples.*)
5. How far did the nobleman walk from Capernaum to Cana to find Jesus? (*Twenty miles.*)
*6. What is the greatest distance that you have ever walked? How long did it take you? (*Allow time for several students to answer.*)
7. What was wrong with the boy? (*He had a fever and was close to death.*)
*8. Were you ever very ill? How did your family react? (*Allow time for several students to share their experiences.*)
9. How did Jesus respond to the father? (*He rebuked him saying, "'Unless you people see miraculous signs and wonders, you will never believe.'"*)
10. Why do you think Jesus acted this way? (*To test the man's faith to determine if it was strong.*)
11. How did the royal official respond? (*"'Sir, come down before my child dies.'"*)
12. Why do you think Jesus did not go to Capernaum? (*He did not want a public display made of the healing event.*)
13. How did the man show his faith? (*He took Jesus at His word. He turned around and started home.*)
14. When did the son recover? (*At the exact time that Jesus told the father that his son would live.*)

15. What do you learn from this? (*It showed that Jesus was involved in the healing.*)

16. What was the result regarding the royal official? (*His entire family believed—the first example in the New Testament of an entire household believing.*)

17. This was the second miracle in Cana. What was the first? (*Jesus changed water to wine at a wedding.*)

18. Why did Jesus perform signs and miracles in the New Testament? (*To show the people that He was the Son of God.*)

*19. Why doesn't Jesus often perform these kinds of miracles today? (*He has given us the Holy Spirit. He delights in faith that does not require proof.*)

*20. Challenge: Find one way to trust Jesus to help you with a problem this coming week.

Activity 1: Extra! Extra! Miracle in Cana

Jesus quietly healed the official's son. If one of today's newspaper reporters were on the scene, this would have been front page coverage.

Ask the students the following: If you were a newspaper reporter covering the event, what would you say in your write-up? Using the Scripture for today, John 4:46-54, allow ten minutes for each member of the class to write a brief lead story for his newspaper. Be sure that everyone has a Bible.

At the end of the time allotted, ask for volunteers to share their stories.

Activity 2: Does Jesus Always Heal?

Divide the class into small groups of three to five students. Ask each group to choose a leader. Allow them ten minutes to discuss the following questions. Then reconvene the class. Ask the leaders to share their group's answers.

1. Does Jesus always heal if we ask? Why not? (*No, some are healed on this earth and some are not. He knows that some individuals can better serve Him without being cured. Perhaps they rely more on His strength.*)

2. Who are some examples of people who asked to be healed and were not? (*Paul in the New Testament, Joni Eareckson Tada who is a quadriplegic artist and author.*)

3. When is everyone healed? (*After death, all believers will be given perfect bodies in heaven.*)

Thoughts for the Day

The leader should summarize the ideas presented in the following thoughts.

The shallow faith of the royal official became a genuine faith in Christ as Lord. This was the first example written in the New Testament of an entire household believing.

In Biblical times, Jesus performed signs and wonders to show the people that He was the Son of God. Yet, today, Christ delights in a faith that does not require signs or miracles. He wants us to believe His word.

Memory Verse

A copy of the memory verse should be made for each student to take home. After the leader distributes the copies, the class can say the verse aloud together.

"Jesus answered, 'The work of God is this: to believe in the one he has sent'" (John 6:29).

Prayer

To conclude the session, the leader leads in prayer, allowing time for individual prayers by the students.

Dear God, thank You for the miracles we are reading in the Bible. Teach us to believe. Help us to trust You with our small problems as well as the big ones. In Jesus' name, amen.

Next Week

The leader briefly mentions the next week's lesson, "A Paralytic Is Placed Before Jesus" (Luke 5:17-26). What happened when some men lowered a paralytic through the roof of a house? How did this show faith? Next week we will study about this unique way of reaching Jesus.

A Paralytic Is Placed Before Jesus

Scripture Text

Luke 5:17-26

Teacher's Tidbits

When the Jews returned to Israel from captivity in Babylon about 440 B.C. under the leadership of Ezra, they formed the Pharisaic party. Thousands of rules emerged. The scribes belonged to this group, and they interpreted the Law for all Pharisees.

Unfortunately, the Pharisees' zeal for the Law often degenerated into superficiality and formality. Although they observed the outward provisions of the Law painstakingly, they violated the real spirit of God's laws in many instances. In their pride, they exalted themselves above the ordinary people. Christ rebuked them and exposed their inconsistencies.

This passage denoted the arrival of the scribes and Pharisees to watch Jesus because His fame had spread. The tragedy was that these Jewish leaders ultimately were responsible for His death.

When the friends tried to bring the paralyzed man through the door, the large crowd would not move aside for the stretcher. The men, convinced that Jesus could heal their friend, probably used an outside stairway to climb onto the roof.

Most Palestinian houses were flat-roofed, composed of beams laid wall-to-wall. The spaces between the beams were packed with twigs, compacted together with mortar, and covered with soil which could be removed easily.

In Biblical times, people believed that if a man suffered, he had sinned. That is why Jesus began by telling the man his sins were forgiven. Without that,

the man would never believe that he could be cured. Here Jesus showed that He not only possessed the power to perform healings, but the power to forgive sins—a right which belonged only to God.

What to Bring

Bibles, a copy of the dramatic reading from Activity 1, and forty balloons for Activity 2.

Questions for Discussion

There may be more than one correct answer for each of the following questions. The leader will ask the questions and wait for the students to provide the answers. The leader should not supply an answer unless it is necessary.

1. Who were the Pharisees? (*A Jewish sect who strictly observed the oral and written Law.*)

2. Who were the scribes? (*The Jewish scholars who interpreted the Law for all Pharisees. They were Pharisees, also.*)

3. Do you remember if these groups were mentioned before in the Bible? (*No, chronologically this is the first time they are mentioned.*)

4. Where did the Pharisees and scribes come from? (*Every village of Galilee, Judea, and Jerusalem.*)

5. Why do you think they came to hear Jesus? (*The fame of Jesus had spread. They wanted to see the carpenter who performed miracles.*)

6. Why did the men have difficulty bringing their paralyzed friend to Jesus? (*The huge crowd would not move aside for the stretcher.*)

7. How would you describe a Palestinian roof? (*Flat with stairs leading to it. It was composed of beams filled in with twigs, compacted with mortar, and covered with soil.*)

8. Do you think a portion of the roof was difficult to remove? (*No, the loosely compacted twigs and soil would have been easy to move.*)

*9. How would you have felt if you were the paralyzed man? (*Allow time for several students to tell what they think it would be like—excited, afraid.*)

10. How would you describe the faith of the friends? (*They cared so much for the paralytic that their faith compelled them to find a way to bring him to Jesus.*)

*11. Has a friend helped you in a similar way? Explain. (*Allow time for as many students as are willing to share on this important subject.*)

*12. Can you give an example of a time when you helped another person? (*Do not force any students who are hesitant to talk about themselves.*)

13. What did the Jews in Biblical times believe caused paralysis and other forms of suffering? (*A per-*

son's sins or those of his father.)

*14. How would you react to the statement today: He is paralyzed because he is bad? (*Paralysis is not a result of anything a person or his family did.*)

*15. How have our sins been conquered today? (*Jesus died on the cross to save us from our sins. If we will only ask, He will forgive us for the things we do wrong.*)

16. Why do you think Jesus first told the paralytic his sins were forgiven instead of telling him he was healed? (*The man probably did not think he could be cured unless his sins were forgiven because of the Jewish tradition.*)

17. Why did Jesus rebuke the Pharisees? (*He could read their thoughts, and He knew they did not recognize His divine power.*)

18. What events in Jesus' life were the Pharisees ultimately responsible for? (*His mock trial and His death on the cross.*)

19. How did the paralyzed man react? (*He stood up, rolled up his mat, and went home praising God.*)

*20. Challenge: Help a friend cope with a problem this coming week.

Activity 1: Don't Drop Me!

Ask a student or a leader to read the following story. Then allow class discussion on how it would feel to be the paralytic on the mat.

This morning, my friends offered to take me to see Jesus. We are on our way now. In front of me, I see a house overflowing with people. My friends try to find an opening through the crowd, but I realize that we'll never be able to reach Jesus by the door. I am so disappointed. He's so close . . . .

But what are my friends doing now? I'm lying in the shade of a sycamore tree while they climb onto the roof. One has taken out his knife and is cutting an opening through the compacted mortar. Now they are removing the twigs and dirt. Surely they don't plan to . . . .

Now they hoist me onto their shoulders. I feel their hands holding me tightly. As we climb the stairs to the roof of the house, I stare at the ground. What if I fall!

My friends carefully set my mat down and tie ropes to the four corners. Gently they lower me through the opening into the presence of Jesus. I have waited for this moment!

Activity 2: Balloon-drop Relay

You need forty or more round, inflated balloons placed in a box. Divide the class into two teams with one person designated to be the "dropper." Each dropper stands on a folding chair with a balloon ready to drop on the floor. The two teams line up in pairs behind each dropper.

Two team members will run in front of the dropper, sit on the floor, back to back, leaving enough room for the balloon to be dropped down between their backs. When the balloon is dropped, they must stand up carefully, keeping the balloon between their backs, and shuffle their way to the finish line on the other side. Upon arrival, the next balloon is dropped to the second pair of each team and so on. If the balloon bursts or drops before reaching the finish line, the pair must return and start over again. No hands may be used to hold onto the balloons. The team to have all of its members reach the finish line first wins.

Thoughts for the Day

The leader should summarize the ideas presented in the following thoughts.

The Pharisees and scribes outwardly observed the Law. Yet, in their pride and conceit, they elevated themselves above ordinary people. Jesus scolded them and exposed their inconsistencies. Ultimately, the Pharisees were responsible for His mock trial and His death on the cross.

In contrast, the paralytic was saved by the faith of his friends. Their determination and eager faith won his cure. And still today, there are individuals who are saved daily by the faith of those who love them.

Memory Verse

A copy of the memory verse should be made for each student to take home. After the leader distributes the copies, the class can say the verse.

"When Jesus saw their faith, he said, 'Friend, your sins are forgiven'" (Luke 5:20).

Prayer

To conclude the session, the leader leads in prayer, allowing time for individual prayers by the students.

Dear Lord, teach us to have faith as great as the friends of the paralytic. Show us how to help others with their problems. In Jesus's name, amen.

Next Week

The leader briefly mentions the next week's lesson, "Matthew Invites Jesus for Dinner" (Matthew 9:9-15). Next week we will study about a hated tax collector who wrote the most widely-read gospel.

Matthew Invites Jesus for Dinner

Scripture Text

Matthew 9:9-15

Teacher's Tidbits

In Biblical Palestine, a tax was levied on everything grown in the ground, on income, and on all goods and commodities as they entered and left the territory of Herod. The Roman government auctioned the right to collect taxes to the highest bidder who was responsible to the Roman government for an agreed sum. Anything he could raise above that amount was his commission. People did not know how much they were legally required to pay in taxes, so the system led to grave abuses. Many a tax collector became wealthy through illegal extortion.

The Jews hated tax collectors, roused by their religious conviction that God alone was King. To pay taxes to any mortal ruler was an infringement of God's rights. Tax collectors were prohibited from the synagogue.

Matthew, a tax collector, was a most unlikely candidate for the office of apostle. Jesus' calling of Matthew is one of the greatest instances of His power to see the possibility of what a person could become.

However, Matthew paid a unique price for answering this call. The other disciples who were fishermen could return to their nets, but for Matthew to leave his post meant no turning back. Once he left the tax office, he could never return to this lucrative business.

What to Bring

Bibles, pencils, paper, a copy of the matching activi-ty from Activity 1 for each student, and a pen, a book, and a ball for each relay team for Activity 2.

Questions for Discussion

There may be more than one correct answer for each of the following question. The leader will ask the questions and wait for the students to provide the answers. The leader should not supply an answer unless it is necessary.

1. What do you know about tax collectors in Biblical times? (*They cheated people by charging too much tax, they often became wealthy.*)

2. How do you think the Jews felt about tax collectors? (*The people hated them and did not allow them in the synagogues; they felt cheated by them.*)

3. How did Matthew respond to Jesus' request to follow Him? (*He left everything and immediately followed Jesus.*)

4. Why do you think Jesus chose Matthew? (*Jesus looked beyond the dishonesty in the job Matthew held and saw the inner man who could glorify Him.*)

*5. Can you give an example of a time when you misjudged someone by his friends or what he wore? (*Allow time for several willing students to share their experiences.*)

*6. What are a person's most important qualities? (*The attitude of his heart; his concern for others; his desire to do good.*)

7. What do you think Matthew gave up to follow Jesus? (*He lost a secure job with a large income.*)

8. What would happen if Matthew tried to return to his former job of tax collecting at a later date? (*Once he left, the Roman government would never have hired him again.*)

*9. What are you willing to give up to follow Christ? (*Allow time for those who are willing to talk on this sensitive subject.*)

10. What did Matthew gain in choosing to follow Jesus? (*Peace of mind, contentment, eternal life.*)

*11. What do we gain when we choose to accept Christ as our Lord and Savior? (*Joy, peace, content-*

ment, fellowship with Christian friends, eternal life.)

12. What did Matthew take with him when he answered Jesus' calling? (*His ability to write.*)

13. How did he use this ability for Christ? (*He wrote the book of Matthew.*)

14. Why do you think Matthew invited his former friends who were tax collectors and sinners to dinner? (*To try to win them to Christ.*)

15. Why did Jesus eat with tax collectors and sinners? (*He came to forgive the sins of those who desperately needed Him.*)

*16. How can we help those individuals today who do not know Christ? (*By being willing to spend time with them, by listening and showing concern.*)

17. How did Jesus answer their question about why His disciples did not fast? (*He said the time was coming when He would be taken away, and then they would fast.*)

18. What did He mean by this statement? (*He was preparing them for His death on the cross.*)

*19. Do you possess a skill or talent that you could use to glorify God? (*Allow time for as many as are willing to speak on this important subject.*)

*20. Challenge: Invite a friend to a social activity at your church this coming week.

Activity 1: Name the Disciples

Match the disciples' names with their descriptions. This can be done individually or by working in teams.

1. The beloved disciple	Judas Iscariot
2. Son of Zebedee (not John)	Matthew
3. Author of the first gospel	John
4. Denied Jesus three times	Thaddaeus
5. Peter's brother	Andrew
6. The doubter	Simon
7. Same person as Bartholemew	James
8. Betrayed Jesus	Nathanael
9. Son of Alphaeus	Peter
10. Also called Jude	Philip
11. The Zealot	James
12. Brought Nathanael to Jesus	Thomas

Solution

1. The beloved disciple	John
2. A son of Zebedee (not John)	James
3. Author of the first Gospel	Matthew
4. Denied Jesus three times	Peter
5. Peter's brother	Andrew
6. The doubter	Thomas
7. Same person as Bartholemew	Nathanael
8. Betrayed Jesus	Judas Iscariot
9. Son of Alphaeus	James

10. Also called Jude	Thaddaeus
11. The Zealot	Simon
12. Brought Nathanael to Jesus	Philip

Activity 2: Pen, Book, and Ball Relay

Divide the group into teams. Each team is given a pen, a tennis ball or other small ball, and a book. Each team member must balance the book on his head, hold the pen in his hands, and grip the ball between his knees. Then he must walk to the finish line and run back to give the items to the next member of the team. The first team to have all its members cross the finish line wins.

Thoughts for the Day

The leader should summarize the ideas presented in the following thoughts.

As a tax collector, Matthew was skilled at writing and keeping records. He used that talent to compose the most-quoted gospel in Christian literature.

Matthew invited his former colleagues to the dinner where Jesus was the guest of honor. No doubt Matthew's purpose was to introduce these men to Christ. We, too, can introduce non-Christians to the Lord if we are willing to spend time with them.

Memory Verse

A copy of the memory verse should be made for each student to take home.

"'As Jesus went on from there, he saw a man named Matthew sitting at the tax collector's booth. "Follow me," he told him, and Matthew got up and followed him'" (Matthew 9:9).

Prayer

To conclude the session, the leader leads in prayer, allowing time for individual prayers by the students.

Dear Lord, teach us to follow You. Show us how to use our talents and abilities to help others and to please You. In Jesus' name, amen.

Next Week

The leader briefly mentions the next week's lesson, "A Centurion's Servant Is Cured" (Luke 7:1-10). What is a centurion? Next week we will study about great faith that amazed Jesus.

A Centurion's Servant Is Cured

Scripture Text

Luke 7:1-10

Teacher's Tidbits

Centurion means "commander of one hundred men." Centurions were the backbone of the Roman army and were often mentioned with respect in the New Testament. The Romans encouraged religion from the cynical motive that it kept the people in order.

Slavery was common in Jesus' time, even among Jews. But the centurion's attitude toward his slave was unusual. Under Roman law, a slave was defined as a living tool who possessed no rights. A master could mistreat or kill him if he chose. Normally when a slave was past working age, he was thrown out to die. This centurion regarded his slave highly, and he decided to approach Jesus for help when the health emergency arose.

The centurion prevented Jesus from coming to his house, because he knew that the strict Jew was forbidden by law from entering the house of a Gentile. Whether the centurion considered Jesus to be the Messiah is not known, but he did look upon Him as being sent by God. The centurion showed great faith in believing that Jesus could control illness as easily as he could control his soldiers and slaves. The episode demonstrates that the Gentiles were included in the circle of those who would benefit from Jesus' love and power. Here is the portrait of a true believer who displayed confidence in God's power to help.

What to Bring

Bibles, pencils, paper, and a copy of the "faith fight" from Activity 1 for each student.

Questions for Discussion

There may be more than one correct answer for each of the following questions. The leader will ask the questions and wait for the students to provide the answers. The leader should not supply an answer unless it is necessary.

1. What was a centurion? (*A commander in the Roman army who usually led approximately one hundred men.*)

2. How did the Romans normally regard their slaves? (*As personal property, they could mistreat or even kill their slaves without penalty.*)

3. How did the centurion treat his slave? (*Valued him highly and went to great lengths to have him healed.*)

4. How did the Romans deal with the Jewish religion? (*They allowed the people to attend the synagogue because it kept them under control.*)

5. What are some of the traits of the centurion? (*Wealthy, thoughtful, humble, generous, kind.*)

6. Why is it surprising that the centurion paid to have the synagogue built? (*He was a Gentile, not a Jew; the expense was tremendous.*)

7. What is a Gentile? (*Any person who is not a Jew.*)

8. How did the Jewish elders regard the centurion? (*They held him in high esteem, said that he loved their nation and built the synagogue.*)

9. How do you think the centurion regarded Jesus? (*He realized Jesus was sent by God; he saw Him as a prophet; he recognized His authority, but he probably did not realize that Jesus was the Messiah.*)

10. Why did the centurion not invite Jesus into his home? (*The strict Jew was forbidden by law from entering the house of a Gentile. Perhaps he did not*

feel worthy of a visit by Jesus.)

11. How did the centurion demonstrate his faith? (*He realized that Jesus did not need to visit his home to heal the servant—that a word from His lips would be sufficient.*)

12. How did the centurion's request differ from the royal official's request in John 4:49 in Lesson 6? (*The royal official begged Jesus to come to his home.*)

13. Which man showed the stronger faith in the power of Jesus? (*The centurion knew with confidence that Jesus could heal his servant without going there.*)

14. What point was the centurion making when he compared his authority over his soldiers and slaves to the power of Jesus? (*He believed that Jesus could control illness as easily as he could control those who followed his command.*)

*15. What is a crisis? (*Allow time for several to give their opinions. A crisis is a disaster, an emergency, a predicament, a difficulty, a problem.*)

*16. Can you tell about an incident when Jesus used His power in your life? (*Allow time for several students to share personal experiences.*)

*17. Can you describe an incident when you prayed that Jesus would help a friend through a crisis? (*Give a number of students time to share on this important question.*)

*18. How strong is your faith regarding the ability of Jesus to work in your daily life? (*Do not force anyone who is not willing to answer on this sensitive issue. You might use a scale from 1 to 10.*)

19. What did Jesus say about the centurion? (*"'I have not found such great faith even in Israel.'"*)

*20. Challenge: This coming week, write a note of encouragement to one friend or relative who is struggling with a crisis.

Activity 1: A Faith Fight

Have the students take turns reading the following definitions of faith. Then allow time to discuss the best ones.

Faith means accepting something as true.
Doesn't faith relieve your doubts?
Faith brings peace with God. And faith is hope.
Yeah! Faith is assurance.
Listen . . . Faith is confidence, conviction, and creed.
But I thought it was trust.
No, it means equipped for victory.
You're all wrong. Faith is the opposite of disbelief.

Faith is all of the above, plus much more. Faith changes lives! Faith changes what you do—how you behave. Your life will be radically changed when you put action into your beliefs because you have a true faith in Jesus Christ.

Activity 2: The Faith Drop

Ask a volunteer to stand on a chair. Have a strong leader stand behind the student and ask him to lean back. Assure the youth that he will be caught. After the student leans back and is caught, ask: When does faith begin? Is faith standing on a chair? Or is faith leaning back?

When the person leans back trusting the one behind him, faith begins. Faith in Christ also involves action. Faith begins when you act on it.

Thoughts for the Day

The leader should summarize the ideas presented in the following thoughts.

The centurion was a respected man who showed sensitivity to those under his command. He demonstrated great faith by believing that Jesus could control illness as easily as he controlled his soldiers and slaves. He realized that Jesus did not need to visit his home to heal his slave.

Here is the portrait of a believer who had confidence in Jesus' power to help. We, too, can benefit from the ability of Jesus to work in our daily lives. The love and authority of Jesus are ours only if we have faith in Him. Let's act on our faith.

Memory Verse

A copy of the memory verse should be made for each student to take home. After the leader distributes the copies, the class can say the verse aloud together.

"'If you have faith as small as a mustard seed, you can say to this mulberry tree, "Be uprooted and planted in the sea," and it will obey you'" (Luke 17:6).

Prayer

To conclude the session, the leader leads the prayer, allowing time for individual prayers by the students.

Dear God, teach us to act on our faith. Please give us confidence to overcome the crises that arise in our lives. In Jesus' name, amen.

Next Week

The leader briefly mentions the next week's lesson, "A Dying Daughter Is Miraculously Healed" (Luke 8:40-42, 49-56). Next week we will study the healing of a girl who was dead.

A Dying Daughter Is Miraculously Healed

Scripture Text

Luke 8:40-42, 49-56

Teacher's Tidbits

The leader should read this section at home before the day of the lesson.

Jairus was president of the synagogue, responsible for its administration and the ordering of public worship. He was wealthy and respected by others. Yet, his most precious possession, his twelve-year-old daughter, was dying.

From the evidence of tombs in ancient Palestine, many were buried alive. Because of climatic conditions and lack of modern embalming methods, most burials took place in a matter of hours after death.

Jairus probably regarded Jesus as a lawbreaker because of the negative attitude of the Jewish religious leaders towards Him. However, Jairus recognized Jesus' ability to perform miracles. He pocketed his pride and asked Jesus for help.

Jairus had to endure some tense moments while the Savior healed the woman. Yet, on the other hand, her miraculous cure proved to Jairus the power of Jesus. Perhaps witnessing this miracle made it easier for Jairus to believe that Jesus would also heal his daughter.

Jesus only allowed His three most intimate followers and the girl's parents to enter the room where she lay. Also, Jesus did not want the parents to lose the deep spiritual significance of the occurrence, so He instructed them to tell no one.

Today, we often think that we can handle all the problems that occur in our lives ourselves. But the way to find the miracles of the grace of God is to pocket our pride, to humbly confess our needs, and to ask for His help.

What to Bring

Bibles, pencils, and paper for Activity 1 for each student.

Questions for Discussion

There may be more than one correct answer for each of the following questions. The leader will ask the questions and wait for the students to provide the answers. The leader should not supply an answer unless it is necessary.

1. Who was Jairus? (*President of the synagogue.*)

2. How do you think the Jews regarded Jairus? (*He was highly respected.*)

3. How do you think Jairus and other leaders of the synagogue felt about Jesus? (*They felt that He broke the law; they feared Him; they did not want Him in their synagogues.*)

4. How do you interpret the act of Jairus falling at Jesus' feet and pleading with Him? (*He swallowed his pride and humbly asked Jesus' help.*)

5. What do we know about the girl? (*She was twelve, Jairus' only daughter, and dying.*)

***6.** Has someone close to you been gravely ill? (*Allow time for those who are willing to talk about this sensitive subject.*)

7. Why do you think Jesus stopped to point out the woman who had touched Him? (*So others would know she was healed, to test the faith of Jairus, to show the woman's faith.*)

***8.** Have you ever asked a friend for a special favor and had him reject you? (*Allow time for several students to express their feelings during such times.*)

9. How do you think Jairus felt when Jesus turned His attention toward the woman? (*Perhaps rejected, abandoned, ignored.*)

10. What positive affect could the woman's healing have had on Jairus? (*Perhaps witnessing this miracle made it easier for Jairus to believe that Jesus would also heal his daughter.*)

11. How did Jesus respond when Jairus was informed that his daughter was dead? (*He said, "'Don't be afraid; just believe, and she will be healed.'"*)

12. Do you think Jairus believed Jesus at this point? Why? (*He did not confront Jesus or question Him; he quietly followed Him into the house. He had just witnessed the healing of another who had been ill for twelve years.*)

13. What did Jesus tell the mourners who were wailing? (*"She is not dead but asleep."*)

14. Do you think she was dead, only sleeping, or in a coma? Why? (*Dead, because verse 55 says that her spirit returned.*)

15. Many were buried alive in ancient Palestine. What is the reason for this? (*Because of the hot climate and lack of modern embalming methods, most burials took place within hours of death; mistakes were made.*)

16. Who did Jesus allow to witness the miracle? (*The parents, Peter, John, and James.*)

17. When the girl stood up, what were Jesus' instructions? (*To give her something to eat.*)

18. What might have been the reason for this? (*She probably needed nourishment; it gave her mother something practical to do when she must have been emotionally exhausted.*)

19. Why did Jesus instruct the parents not to tell anyone? (*He did not want the parents to lose the deep spiritual significance of the situation.*)

*20. Challenge: This coming week, think about a time when you felt rejected. Ask Jesus to help you deal with your feelings.

Activity 1: Letters to Jesus

Have each student take a piece of paper and a pencil. Have the class imagine that they are writing a letter to Jesus. Assure them that these letters are personal, and they will not be asked to read their letters.

Suggest that the letter start with a greeting. It could include some "thank you's." Share some experiences and feelings with Him. Describe some problems and concerns and ask help dealing with them.

Allow about ten minutes for the students to write the letters. Then explain that these letters are just like prayers, and Jesus listens to them. The letters are to be taken home and read privately.

Activity 2: Bang, You're Out

The leader knows the secret in this game, and

everyone else is trying to guess how it is done. Everyone should be seated around the room in a casual manner. Standing up front, the leader raises his hand, points it at a student, and says, "Bang, you're out." He then asks the group to guess who he shot. It is rarely the person who he pointed his finger at.

Several people will guess, but they will usually be wrong. Then you announce who you actually shot. The first person to speak after you say, "Bang, you're out" is the person you actually shot. If a student guesses the secret, have him whisper it to the leader. If he is right, let him take over as shooter until another student figures it out.

Thoughts for the Day

The leader should summarize the ideas presented in the following thoughts.

As president of the synagogue, Jairus knew that Jesus was regarded as a lawbreaker. Yet, his only daughter lay dying. He pocketed his pride and came humbly to Jesus because he knew Jesus possessed the power to help him.

Today, we often think we can handle all the problems that occur in our lives. But we can't. We need to pocket our pride, too. If we humbly confess our needs to God, He will answer our prayers. Sometimes the answers are not exactly what we had in mind, but He always listens and answers.

Memory Verse

A copy of the memory verse should be made for each student to take home. After the leader distributes the copies, the class can say the verse aloud together.

"'So I say to you: Ask and it will be given to you; seek and you will find; knock and the door will be opened to you. For everyone who asks receives; he who seeks finds; and to him who knocks, the door will be opened'" (Luke 11:9, 10).

Prayer

To conclude the session, the leader leads in prayer, allowing time for individual prayers by the students.

Dear Lord, help us to forget our pride and come humbly to You. Teach us to ask You to help us solve the problems in our lives. In Jesus' name, amen.

Next Week

The leader briefly mentions the next week's lesson, "A Woman Touches Jesus' Cloak" (Luke 8:43-48). Next week we will study about a woman who was healed by touching the edge of Jesus' cloak.

LESSON 11

A Woman Touches Jesus' Cloak

Scripture Text

Luke 8:43-48

Teacher's Tidbits

The leader should read this section at home before the day of the lesson.

In Biblical times all devout Jews wore robes with fringes on them. The fringes ended on the corners with tassels of white thread woven with blue thread. These tassels represented the commandments of God and reminded the Jew every time he dressed that he was a man of God. Today the tassels still exist on the prayer shawl that a Jew wears around his head and shoulders. The woman, who forced her way through the multitude to reach Jesus, touched one of those tassels on His garment.

According to the Jewish ideas of that time, the woman was considered an outcast because of her bleeding. She could not take part in religious proceedings, could not go into the temple, could not touch others, and was separated from her husband.

For Jesus, the woman was someone in need. He mentally blocked out the crowd and gave His complete attention to her.

If her cure had taken place without the Savior making it known publicly, the inhabitants of the town would have continued to show scorn and prejudice as they had for years. Jesus knew her needs and sorrows. He understood her circumstances, so He made her appear before the multitude to testify publicly that she was healed.

What to Bring

Bibles, pencils, paper, a copy of the discrimination questions from Activity 1 for each small group, and blindfolds for Activity 2 for everyone.

Questions for Discussion

There may be more than one correct answer for each of the following questions. The leader will ask the questions and wait for the students to provide the answers. The leader should not supply an answer unless it is necessary.

1. What was the medical problem of the woman who touched Jesus? (*She had bled for twelve years.*)

2. How was the number twelve mentioned in last week's lesson? (*Jairus' daughter was twelve years old when Jesus healed her.*)

3. Do you think the woman had searched for ways to be healed? (*Some texts say that she spent all her money on doctors.*)

4. Because of her bleeding, the woman was considered an outcast. What did this mean in biblical society? (*She could not go to the temple; she could not touch others; she was separated from her husband; she could not be a part of social gatherings.*)

*5. What are some of the ways we greet each other today? (*Hand shakes, hugs, holding hands.*)

*6. How would you feel if you were considered an outcast and were not allowed to go public places or to talk to other people? (*Allow time for several students to share on this hypothetical situation. Lonely, afraid, bored, unwanted.*)

7. What part of Jesus' cloak did the woman touch? (*The tassel on the corner.*)

8. What significance did the tassels have for the Jew? (*They represented the commandments and reminded him that he belonged to God.*)

9. Have you seen a Jewish prayer shawl today? If so, describe it. (*It has tassels on each corner with blue and white threads woven through the tassel.*)

10. What happened when the woman touched Jesus? (*Her bleeding immediately stopped.*)

11. Why did Jesus ask, "'Who touched me?'" (*Because people needed to know that the cure had taken place so they would not show the woman scorn and treat her like an outcast anymore.*)

12. When the woman realized she could not go unnoticed, how did she react? (*She came trembling and fell at Jesus' feet.*)

13. How would you compare her meeting of Jesus with that of Jairus? (*Both fell at His feet; the woman had already been healed, and Jairus pleaded for his daughter's life.*)

14. How would you contrast the woman with Jairus?

(*Jairus was popular, wealthy, respected, and held a high position. The woman was an outcast, destitute, rejected by everyone in her town.*)

*15. How would you have felt if you were Jairus when Jesus appeared to ignore his plea and turned to the outcast? (*Rejected, impatient, ignored, cast aside, forgotten.*)

16. Yet, why did Jesus suddenly turn His attention to the woman? (*He knew He could heal Jairus' daughter anytime, and He wanted to teach a lesson on faith and make the people aware that the woman was no longer unclean.*)

17. Why did Jesus say, "'Your faith has healed you'"? (*He did not want her to think it was some magical power from touching His cloak; He wanted others to see her faith.*)

*18. Why do you think Jesus called her daughter? (*He was including her in the family of God; she was Jewish; and perhaps He was drawing a parallel between her and the daughter of Jairus He would soon bring back to life.*)

*19. Have you ever come to Jesus in prayer and felt that He gave you His undivided attention? (*Allow time for as many students as wish to share their experiences.*)

*20. Challenge: Give a friend or a family member your undivided attention some time during the coming week.

Activity 1: Discrimination

Divide the class into small groups of three to five students. Ask each group to choose a leader. Allow the students ten minutes to discuss the following questions. Then reconvene the class. Ask the leaders to share their group's answers.

1. Are there students at your school who are considered outcasts?

2. Is this discrimination based on race, sex, or actions?

3. What could you do as a Christian to help these individuals' self-esteem?

4. What could you say to make them feel needed?

Activity 2: Blind Sardines

One person is appointed or volunteers to be the sardine. The sardine does not wear a blindfold, but all the other participants wear blindfolds. Their objective is to come in contact with the sardine.

When a person wearing a blindfold touches another person, he asks that student if he is the sardine. The sardine must say "yes" if touched. Once an individual runs into the sardine, he holds onto the sardine for the remainder of the game. A chain of people is gradually formed. Anyone who touches anyone in the chain becomes part of the chain of sardines. The game ends when everyone belongs to the chain of sardines.

Thoughts for the Day

The leader should summarize the ideas presented in the following thoughts.

A woman forced her way through the crowd to touch the tassel on Jesus' cloak. She was healed instantly, but Jesus wanted the village people to realize that she should no longer be considered an outcast.

Jesus stopped and turned His full attention to the woman. God loves each one of us individually, and He gives us His undivided attention when we come to Him in prayer.

Memory Verse

A copy of the memory verse should be made for each student to take home. After the leader distributes the copies, the class can say the verse aloud together.

"'Let them give thanks to the Lord for his unfailing love and his wonderful deeds for men'" (Psalm 107:15).

Prayer

To conclude the session, the leader leads in prayer, allowing time for individual prayers by the students.

Dear God, we praise You for giving each of us Your individual attention. Thank You for loving us and healing our hurts. In Jesus' name, amen.

Next Week

The leader briefly mentions the next week's lesson, "Peter Walks on Water" (Matthew 14:22-33). Why were the disciples afraid of Jesus? Why did they fear for their lives? Next week we will study about what happened when Peter took his eyes off the Lord.

Peter Walks on Water

Scripture for Text

Matthew 14:22-33

Teacher's Tidbits

The leader should read this section at home before the day of the lesson.

The Sea of Galilee is noted for its sudden and violent storms. These are caused by cold air sweeping down from the barren plateaus, through the ravines, and converging on the lake. A sail is useless in the high winds and tossing waves.

Blown far from their destination, the disciples strained at the oars, fearing for their lives. They were on the sea, battling the waves for at least nine hours. In the panic of the night, they forgot Jesus' assurance that their Heavenly Father understood their needs.

Jesus knew of their situation long before it happened, so He did not rush away from prayer to help them. But when Jesus finally went to the disciples, He brought them an inward peace and a deeper faith as well as outer calm. This was the first time the twelve declared their Master to be the Son of God.

Peter often acted on impulse, without counting the cost. He was ruled by his heart which was always filled with love, even though he sometimes failed. Every time Peter reached a moment of failure, he clutched at Christ and regained his footing. His failures strengthened his faith and brought him closer to Jesus Christ.

At times, life can be a desperate struggle with our circumstances, our temptations, our sorrows, and our decisions. But we need not struggle alone because Jesus comes to us across the storms of life, with His hands outstretched, telling us to have no fear. If we rely on Him, our faith is strengthened by these difficult times.

What to Bring

Bibles, pencils, paper, a copy of "Places to Pray" from Activity 1 for each student, and a copy of the questions from Activity 2 dealing with fear for each small group.

Questions for Discussion

There may be more than one correct answer for each of the following questions. The leader will ask the questions and wait for the students to provide the answers. The leader should not supply an answer unless it is necessary.

1. Why do you think Jesus did not go with the disciples in the boat? (*He needed some time to Himself, some time to pray.*)

2. Where did Jesus go and why? (*He went alone to a mountainside to pray to His Heavenly Father.*)

*3. How much time do you take daily to spend alone with your Heavenly Father? (*Allow time for those who are willing to answer. Ask everyone to think about the question silently.*)

*4. What are some of the ways you can spend time alone with God? (*By praying, by reading the Bible, by stopping and listening to Him speak.*)

5. How strong do you suppose the storm was? (*The wind was raging and had blown them into the center of the lake; they could not row; they had no control over their boat.*)

6. How long had they been fighting the storm? (*At least nine hours; it was dark.*)

7. What do you think the disciples felt during the storm? (*They were afraid; they felt helpless; they thought of the danger; in their panic they forgot Jesus' assurance.*)

8. Do you think Jesus could see them struggling from His place of prayer? (*He probably could not physically see them, but He knew what was happening.*)

9. Why didn't Jesus go immediately to His disciples when the storm began? (*He was probably tired; He wanted to teach them a lesson, and He needed time alone in prayer with God.*)

10. Why didn't the disciples recognize Jesus when He went to them? (*Perhaps because it was dark; they did not grasp the fact that He could walk on water; they were scared.*)

11. What did Jesus say to them? (*"Don't be afraid."*)

*12. During what incident in your life were you most afraid? (*Allow time for as many students as are willing* *to speak on this important problem.)*

*13. What did you do to overcome your fear? (*Allow several students to share their solutions.*)

*14. What does Jesus say to us about being afraid? (*He is always by our side so we need never be afraid.*)

15. Why do you think Peter wanted to walk on the water? (*As a way to get to Jesus.*)

16. When did Peter begin to sink? (*When he took his eyes off Jesus, when he watched the waves instead.*)

17. How would you describe Peter's faith? (*Peter's failures and difficulties brought him closer to Jesus. His faith was strong because he depended on his Lord.*)

*18. What happened to your faith during a difficult situation? (*Allow time for several students to respond. Hopefully your faith was strengthened.*)

19. What did the disciples say when Jesus calmed the storm? (*"Truly you are the Son of God."*)

*20. Challenge: Think of something you are afraid of, and ask Jesus to help you overcome your fears this coming week.

Activity 1: Places to Pray

We can talk to God anytime, anywhere, about anything we want to. Here are some suggested locations. Rank them from 1 to 20, with 1 being your first choice. Allow ten minutes for the students to write down their answers. Then discuss the different places they can pray.

AT A PARTY	ON YOUR ROOF
ON THE MOON	ON A DESERT
ON A MOUNTAIN TOP	AT THE BEACH
IN YOUR CLOSET	IN YOUR FAVORITE CHAIR
AT THE DENTIST	WHILE DOING HOMEWORK
IN CHURCH	IN YOUR BACK YARD
ON YOUR BIKE	IN THE CAR
IN A PHONE BOOTH	AT THE LIBRARY
ON A SURFBOARD	ON SKIS
ON A SKATEBOARD	IN BED

WHO NEEDS A LIFE JACKET WHEN YOU'VE GOT JESUS.

Activity 2: Dealing With Fear

Divide the class into small groups of three to five students. Have them discuss the following questions for five to ten minutes. The results will not be shared with the class.

1. Are you often afraid?

2. Do you know what causes this fear?

3. How have you tried to cope with the problem?

4. Have you prayed about the fear? With what results?

Thoughts for the Day

The leader should summarize the ideas presented in the following thoughts.

Peter acted on impulse. He jumped out of the boat and walked on the water. But when he took his eyes off Jesus and stared at the raging waves, he began to sink. His faith was enough to get him out of the boat, but not enough to carry him across the water. Yet, when he reached out to Jesus again, Jesus calmed the storm and Peter's fears.

Jesus comes to us across the storms of life with His hands outstretched. Ultimately, Peter's faith was strengthened by his ordeal as was that of the other disciples. Jesus wants our faith to grow when we are struggling with problems and decisions.

Memory Verse

A copy of the memory verse should be made for each student to take home. After the leader distributes the copies, the class can say the verse aloud together.

"But Jesus immediately said to them: 'Take courage! It is I. Don't be afraid'" (Matthew 14:27).

Prayer

To conclude the session, the leader leads in prayer, allowing time for individual prayers by the students.

Dear Lord, thank You for always being available when we need You. In Jesus' name, amen.

Next Week

The leader briefly mentions the next week's lesson, "The Canaanite Woman's Daughter Is Healed" (Matthew 15:21-28). Next week we will study about a trip Jesus took to a foreign land.

The Canaanite Woman's Daughter Is Healed

Scripture Text

Matthew 15:21-28

Teacher's Tidbits

The leader should read this section at home before the day of the lesson.

The end was near. There was no place in Palestine where Jesus was safe from the malignant hostility of the scribes and Pharisees. So He went north to the land of Tyre and Sidon where the Phoenicians (or Canaanites) lived. Jesus had no commission from the Father to open a ministry among the Gentiles. He sought rest and privacy, a time of deliberate withdrawal with His disciples to prepare them for the day of His crucifixion.

The Canaanite woman was raised in a pagan culture known for its wickedness. The Canaanites were the ancestral enemies of the Jews. The woman didn't know God's Word, but her faith grew by contact with Jesus. She publicly affirmed His power over her former gods of wood and stone.

Great faith does not give up, nor is it deterred by obstacles or disappointments. The story illustrates the power of prevailing prayer when coupled with implicit faith. How many times Christians have not because they ask not. This occasion when Jesus was outside the Jewish territory foreshadowed the broadcast of the gospel to the whole world.

What to Bring

Bibles, pencils, paper, and a copy of the matching activity from Activity 1 for each student.

Questions for Discussion

There may be more than one correct answer for each of the following questions. The leader will ask the questions and wait for the students to provide the answers. The leader should not supply an answer unless it is necessary.

1. Why do you think Jesus left Palestine? (*To escape the crowds and the hostile Pharisees, to get some rest, to be alone with His disciples and prepare them for His crucifixion.*)

2. Who lived in Tyre and Sidon? (*The Phoenicians or Canaanites, Gentiles who worshipped many gods and were the ancestral enemies of the Jews.*)

3. What is a Gentile? (*A person who is not a Jew.*)

4. What did the woman say to Jesus? (*"'Lord, Son of David, have mercy on me! My daughter is suffering terribly from demon-possession.'"*)

5. How did Jesus react? (*He ignored her.*)

6. How would you have expected Him to react? (*To show her compassion, to heal her immediately.*)

7. What was the disciples' suggestion for the woman? (*To send her away, they saw her as a nuisance.*)

*8. Contrast their reaction with what you would consider a Christian response? (*They did not show love, pity, concern, or compassion.*)

9. What does Jesus answer? (*"'I was sent only to the lost sheep of Israel.'"*)

10. What does Jesus mean by this unusual reply? (*His first priority was to the Jews. He did not feel God was calling Him to a ministry of the Gentiles at that time.*)

11. What did the woman know about Jesus before meeting Him? (*She knew of Jesus' healing power, that King David was His ancestor. She addressed Him with reverent respect.*)

12. Why did Jesus keep asking the woman questions? (*He set up a series of barriers to test her faith.*)

13. What characteristics did she show? (*She was not discouraged, she showed love for her daughter; and she was persistent.*)

14. What obstacles did the woman's faith have to overcome? (*It moved beyond ethnic and cultural obstacles, bypassed ritual religion, and affirmed Jesus' power over gods of wood and stone.*)

15. What change do you see in the woman as the conversation progresses? (*Her faith grew while in contact with Jesus; she knelt before Him and said, "'Lord, help me.'"*)

16. Why did Jesus ultimately grant her request? (*Because she showed great faith even though she had never read the scriptures.*)

***17.** What are some of the qualities of great faith people show today? (*They do not give up; they are not deterred by obstacles or disappointments.*)

***18.** Who is an example of a person whom you admire? (*Allow time for several students to tell about these people.*)

***19.** Who has affected your life because of his great faith? (*Do not force any students who are not willing to share on this personal subject.*)

***20.** Challenge: Be friendly to someone at school this coming week whom you usually do not talk to.

Activity 1: Match Negative to Positive

The column of words on the left is filled with positive words; the column on the right with negative antonyms. Match the word on the left with the opposite meaning on the right.

POSITIVE	HOSTILE
BROADCAST	NEGATIVE
LAUGH	DISCRIMINATE
PERSIST	SUPPRESS
ACCEPT EVERYONE	DISAPPOINT
PEACEFUL	WITHDRAW
ANSWER	MALIGNANT
FULFILL	QUESTION
ADVANTAGE	CRY
BENIGN	OBSTACLE

Solution

POSITIVE	NEGATIVE
BROADCAST	SUPPRESS
LAUGH	CRY
PERSIST	WITHDRAW
ACCEPT EVERYONE	DISCRIMINATE
PEACEFUL	HOSTILE
ANSWER	QUESTION
FULFILL	DISAPPOINT
ADVANTAGE	OBSTACLE
BENIGN	MALIGNANT

Activity 2: Canaanite Chain Tag

Choose one student to tag people. When he catches someone, the two of them join hands and continue catching people as a unit. Once there are eight in the group, the chain breaks in half, and two sets of four try to catch the remaining people. The game continues until everyone is caught.

Thoughts for the Day

The leader should summarize the ideas presented in the following thoughts.

The incident of healing the Canaanite's daughter was the beginning of broadcasting the gospel to the whole world. The woman turned from her idols of stone and wood to serve the living God. She did not give up when Jesus tested her.

Great faith does not give up, nor is it discouraged by obstacles or disappointments. How many times our requests are not granted because we do not come to God in prayer.

Memory Verse

A copy of the memory verse should be made for each student to take home. After the leader distributes the copies, the class can say the verse aloud together.

"'Until now you have not asked for anything in my name. Ask and you will receive, and your joy will be complete'" (John 16:24).

Prayer

To conclude the session, the leader leads in prayer, allowing time for individual prayers by the students.

Dear Lord, please help us to have great faith like the Canaanite woman. Teach us to make our requests known to You, realizing that Your will for our lives needs to be done. In Jesus' name, amen.

Next Week

The leader briefly mentions the next week's lesson, "A Blind Man Receives His Sight" (John 9:1-34). Who was the blind beggar who received his sight? Why did Jesus tell him to wash in the pool of Siloam? Next week we will study about a beggar who asked the Pharisees if they wanted to become Jesus' disciples, too.

LESSON 14

A Blind Man Receives His Sight

Scripture Text

John 9:1-34

Teacher's Tidbits

This is the only miracle in the gospels in which the sufferer was afflicted from birth. Both the disciples and authorities interpreted this congenital blindness as evidence of sin. The idea that children inherit the consequences of their parents' sin is woven into the thought of the Old Testament.

By making clay with dust and spittle, Jesus was guilty of working on the Sabbath. A person could not even extinguish a lamp or light a fire on the Sabbath. Also, it was forbidden by law to help someone on the Sabbath unless the situation was life-threatening.

The Pool of Siloam, a landmark in Jerusalem, was one of the greatest engineering feats of the ancient world. The water supply for Jerusalem came from a fountain located 583 miles away which in the event of siege could be completely cut off. Hezekiah's men cut a conduit through the solid rock from the spring into the city forming the Pool of Siloam. Siloam means "sent." The water for the Feast of Tabernacles was drawn from this pool.

What to Bring

Bibles, pencils, paper, several blindfolds or an old sheet and items to use as obstacles for Activity 2, and a copy of the matching activity from Activity 1 for each student.

Questions for Discussion

There may be more than one correct answer for each of the following questions. The leader will ask the questions and wait for the students to provide the answers. The leader should not supply an answer unless it is necessary.

1. How long had the man been blind? (*Since birth.*)

2. Can you recall another healing where the sufferer had been afflicted since birth? (*No, this is the only one.*)

3. The disciples assumed that sin had caused the man's blindness. How did Jesus answer them? (*Neither the man nor his parents sinned to cause the problem.*)

4. What did Jesus say was the purpose of the blindness? (*To show the glory and power of God in action.*)

5. What did Jesus mean by, "As long as it is day, we must do the work of him who sent me"? (*Jesus needed to finish God's work in the short time before His crucifixion; the disciples needed to tell others about Jesus while they were still alive.*)

*6. How can you do God's work today? (*Allow time for several students to speak. By helping a friend, by telling someone about Jesus.*)

*7. What is the danger of putting off helping someone or not doing something you know God wants you to do? (*Tomorrow may be too late; you may never get a second chance.*)

8. What did Jesus mean by the words, "Night is coming"? (*Perhaps the hours of darkness while He was on the cross, perhaps the battle with evil that all believers face, perhaps literal darkness that comes at night.*)

9. Why did Jesus call Himself, "the light of the world?" (*Those who follow Him will not walk in darkness but will have eternal life.*)

10. Why do you think Jesus used dust and spittle to form the clay to place over the blind man's eyes? (*Jesus often used natural substances to perform miracles; He wanted to use action to confirm the man's faith.*)

*11. Have you ever burned your finger? How did you react? (*Stuck it in your mouth to allow the saliva to sooth it.*)

12. How did the man show his faith? (*He obeyed without hesitation and went to the Pool of Siloam where he received his gift of sight.*)

13. Why were the Pharisees angry because Jesus healed the man? (*They were not allowed to work, to heal, or to even light a lamp on the Sabbath.*)

14. Why wouldn't the blind man's parents answer the Pharisees questions? (*The Pharisees could excommunicate the parents from the synagogue; this would cause them to be shunned by other Jews.*)

15. What did the man say to the Pharisees the second time he was summoned? (*"I was blind, but now I see. Do you want to become His disciples, too?"*)

16. How do you see faith develop in the man? (*He knew Jesus was a prophet, and he obeyed Him. But as he spoke to the Pharisees, he realized that Jesus must be sent from God.*)

17. What statement of the man best shows his faith? (*"If this man were not from God, he could do nothing."*)

*18. What is spiritual blindness today? (*Those who do not believe in Jesus cannot see His love for them.*)

*19. What does helping others show about God? (*To help someone in need shows that God is working inside of us.*)

*20. Challenge: Think about how you can help a person with a disability.

Activity 1: Match the Healing Miracles

So far in our lessons Jesus has performed seven healings. Divide the group into teams of three to five students. Have them match the titles on the left with the Bible verses on the right. The first team to finish wins if their answers are correct.

TITLES	VERSES
The Canaanite Woman's Daughter	Luke 8:40-42, 49-56
An Official's Sick Son	Luke 8:43-48
A Blind Man	Matthew 15:21-28
A Paralytic	John 9:1-34
A Centurion's Servant	Luke 5:17-26
A Bleeding Woman	John 4:46-54
Jairus' Daughter	Luke 7:1-10

Solution

TITLES	VERSES
The Canaanite Woman's Daughter	Matthew 15:21-28
An Official's Sick Son	John 4:46-54
A Blind Man	John 9:1-34
A Paralytic	Luke 5:17-26
A Centurion's Servant	Luke 7:1-10
A Bleeding Woman	Luke 8:43-48
Jairus' Daughter	Luke 8:40-42, 49-56

Activity 2: Guiding the Blind

This activity shows how difficult it can be for a blind person to travel. The game is designed to illustrate how some people give good advice and others give bad advice.

Have the blindfolded person wait outside the door while the class sets up the room with a variety of obstacles such as pop bottles, cans, chairs so that someone would have to avoid them in order to walk across the room. The object is for the blindfolded person to walk across the room without knocking over any of the obstacles.

Assign one student to be a foe and one to be a friend to the blindfolded person. They will offer advice as he tries to cross the room. The blindfolded person must determine who is giving good advice and who is giving bad advice. Rearrange the room and reassign the roles of friend and foe for each student who is blindfolded.

Thoughts for the Day

The leader should summarize the ideas presented in the following thoughts.

The blind beggar received his sight by obeying Jesus and washing in the Pool of Siloam. At first, he thought Jesus was only a prophet, but as his faith developed he proclaimed, "'If this man were not from God, he could do nothing.'" Finally, he boldly asked the Pharisees if they wanted to become Jesus' disciples, too.

Jesus said that all His followers need to do God's work while there is still time. We should never put off until tomorrow what we can do for God or others today, because another opportunity may never come.

Memory Verse

A copy of the memory verse should be made for each student to take home. After the leader distributes the copies, the class can say the verse.

"When Jesus spoke again to the people, he said, 'I am the light of the world. Whoever follows me will never walk in darkness, but will have the light of life'" (John 8:12).

Prayer

To conclude the session, the leader leads in prayer, allowing time for individual prayers by the students.

Dear Lord, teach us not to put off things that we should do today. Show us how to express concern and love by helping others. In Jesus' name, amen.

Next Week

The leader briefly mentions the next week's lesson, "Martha Receives Instructions From Jesus" (Luke 10:38-42). Next week we will study about two sisters who were very different.

Martha Receives Instructions From Jesus

Scripture Text

Luke 10:38-42

Teacher's Tidbits

Jesus turned to His friends in Bethany to find an oasis of calm away from the demanding crowds. Jesus was on His way to Jerusalem, to face His crucifixion.

Martha, motivated by hospitality and love for the Lord, became deeply involved in her preparations to make the time special for Jesus. She rushed around cleaning and cooking. But the task was evidently too much for her, and she demonstrated reproach for Mary in her voice. The harmony between Martha and the others was shattered.

Jesus did not criticize Martha's activities but her wrong attitude. Martha's service was characterized by anxiety and stress. If she had planned a simpler meal, she could have listened to Jesus as Mary did. She had few opportunities left to spend time with Him. The food would last only a short time, but what Mary learned would last a lifetime.

What to Bring

Bibles, pencils, paper, three copies of the skit from Activity 2, a broom, and a dust rag.

Questions for Discussion

There may be more than one correct answer for each of the following questions. The leader will ask the questions and wait for the students to provide the answers. The leader should not supply an answer unless it is necessary.

1. Where were Jesus and His disciples going and why? (*The Passover in Jerusalem, two miles away.*)

2. Who did He stop in Bethany to visit? (*His friends—Mary, Martha, and Lazarus.*)

3. What was Martha doing after Jesus arrived? (*Rushing around preparing an elaborate meal.*)

4. Was this what Jesus wanted? (*No, He wanted a peaceful, quiet visit with His friends.*)

5. Was what Martha did wrong? Explain. (*No, her attitude was wrong, not what she did.*)

*6. Have you ever thought you knew what someone needed, but discovered you were totally wrong? Explain. (*Allow time for as many students as are willing to share on this thought-provoking question.*)

7. What was Mary doing while Martha prepared the meal? (*Sitting at Jesus' feet, listening to His words.*)

8. Should she have helped prepare the meal? Explain. (*No, a simple meal would have been adequate.*)

9. How did Martha react to what Mary was doing? (*She scolded her; Martha disturbed the harmony between herself and her sister.*)

10. How did Jesus react to Martha's outburst? (*He was tender and instructive; He wanted her to see her wrong attitude; He did not want her to miss this opportunity to listen to Him.*)

11. What did Jesus mean by "'only one thing is needed'"? (*Spending time with Him was most important.*)

12. What does Jesus mean by the words, "'Mary has chosen what is better, and it will not be taken away from her'"? (*What Mary learned from listening to Jesus would stay in her mind long after Jesus ascended into Heaven.*)

*13. Did Jesus mean that active service is unimportant? Explain. (*No, personal worship with Him is more important, but actions are important, too.*)

14. What are some of the personality traits of Martha? (*Active, energetic, hard-working.*)

15. What are some of the characteristics of Mary? (*Contemplative, quiet, good listener.*)

*16. What are some of your personality characteristics? (*Allow time for as many students as are willing to speak.*)

*17. How do you get along with others at school who have very different personalities from your own? (*Allow time for several students to talk about their experiences at school.*)

*18. Do your closest friends have similar personalities or very different ones from your own? (*Give several students a chance to answer.*)

*19. Do you become so busy with outward activities that you neglect a quiet worship time with God? (*This is best answered silently.*)

*20. Challenge: Stop and find a quiet worship time this week when you can listen as Jesus speaks to you.

Activity 1: Personality Traits

Write the following three personality headings on the chalkboard. Ask the students to list personality characteristics under the following three categories. Assure them that this is a private list. They will not be asked to share their list with the class.

My Traits   **Wished-For Traits**   **Traits I Admire**

Activity 2: A Visit to Bethany Skit

Assign the three speaking parts of the skit to one boy and two girls. Allow time for them to read through their parts before the performance begins. If the group is small, have everyone enter with Jesus and sit around Him. If the group is too large, have several disciples enter with Jesus and the rest of the students can form the audience.

Martha: (*Dust rag in her hand.*) Hurry, Mary! Jesus will be here any minute, and there's so much to do. There's SO much to do. (*Martha scurries around dusting everything in sight.*)

Mary: (*Stands dreamily leaning on a broom.*) It will be so wonderful having our friend Jesus here. (*She sighs, sweeps one or two strokes and leans on the broom again.*)

Martha: Hurry up with that sweeping, Mary. Don't you know He will be here any minute?

Mary: (*Sweeps a little and leans on the broom again.*) Jesus always says so many interesting things. I learn so much by listening to His words.

Martha: (*Frowns at Mary.*) I don't have time to stand here and discuss this. I'm going into the kitchen to check the lamb and all the trimmings. This will be the greatest feast that Jesus has ever eaten. (*She leaves.*)

(*Jesus arrives and knocks at the door. Mary throws down her broom and lets Him in.*)

Mary: Welcome, Jesus. Come in and rest your feet. Hello, everyone.

(*The disciples enter with Jesus, acknowledge Mary's hello, and sit down around Jesus. Mary sits at His feet.*)

Martha: (*Enters the room.*) Lord, don't you care that my sister made me do all the work myself? Tell her to help me!

Jesus: Martha, Martha, you are worried and upset about many things, but only one thing is needed. Mary has chosen to sit and listen to me. Come, sit down next to your sister and listen to my words.

(*Everyone exits.*)

Thoughts for the Day

The leader should summarize the ideas presented in the following thoughts.

Jesus came to Bethany for a quiet visit with His friends on the way to Jerusalem. Martha was so busy making elaborate plans for a great feast that she forgot to actually sit down and spend time with Jesus. Jesus knew they would not have many more visits like this one.

We, too, need to be careful not to busy ourselves with outward activities to the extent that we neglect the quiet worship of the Lord.

Memory Verse

A copy of the memory verse should be made for each student to take home. After the leader distributes the copies, the class can say the verse.

"'And that you may love the Lord your God, listen to his voice, and hold fast to him. For the Lord is your life'" (Deuteronomy 30:20).

Prayer

To conclude the session, the leader leads in prayer, allowing time for individual prayers by the students.

Dear Lord, teach us to be quiet so we can listen to You. Help us not to clutter up our lives with so many activities that we shut You out. In Jesus' name, amen.

Next Week

The leader briefly mentions the next week's lesson, "A Rich Young Man Meets Jesus" (Luke 18:18-28). Next week we will study about a young man who walked away sad.

A Rich Young Man Meets Jesus

Scripture Text

Luke 18:18-28

Teacher's Tidbits

The leader should read this section at home before the day of the lesson.

The rich youth was a leading personality among the Jews in his area, but he knew within his heart that something was lacking. The young ruler wanted to inherit eternal life through his own good actions, so Jesus referred him to the Ten Commandments. No one, except Jesus, has led a perfect life.

The young man sincerely believed that he had kept the commandments. The Savior did not express His opinion on the truth of the young man's claim. Instead He looked into the youth's heart and saw one great obstacle. He had become so attached to his earthly possessions that a barrier had arisen between him and God.

The secret and the tragedy of the rich ruler was that he loved his money and personal possessions more than he loved God. That is why Jesus told him to give it all away. If he was to find happiness, he needed to learn to live for others with the same intensity that he had lived for himself.

No one is able, in his own strength, to overcome the temptation of earthly wealth. The rich ruler left sad and presumably unsaved.

Jesus only asks us to give up the things that hamper our spiritual growth. He does not usually call upon us to sell our belongings or leave our families. What He wants most of all is for us to surrender first place in our hearts and lives to Him.

What to Bring

Bibles, pencils, paper, and copies of the pictionary words from Activity 2 for each table of students.

Questions for Discussion

There may be more than one correct answer for each of the following questions. The leader will ask the questions and wait for the students to provide the answers. The leader should not supply an answer unless it is necessary.

1. What was the rich ruler's first question? (*"'Good teacher, what must I do to inherit eternal life?'"*)

2. Why did Jesus ask the ruler, "'Why do you call me good?'" (*Jesus did not want a superficial, flattering greeting from someone who regarded Him as an ordinary human.*)

3. Who did the young man think Jesus was? (*A good teacher, perhaps John the Baptist, Elijah, or Jeremiah, but he regarded Jesus as human not as God's Son.*)

4. What did the young man say about the commandments? (*He claimed he had kept them since he was a small boy.*)

*5. What would you have said to the young man at this point? (*Allow time for several student to express their opinions. No one can keep all the commandments all the time.*)

6. Has anyone successfully kept all the commandments all of his life? (*No, only Jesus has.*)

7. Why didn't Jesus set the young ruler straight on this point? (*This was not the issue that Jesus wanted to deal with.*)

8. How was the youth trying to gain eternal life? (*Through his own efforts, without the help of Jesus.*)

*9. How do we gain eternal life? (*When we believe in Jesus, trust Him as our Savior, and ask forgiveness of our sins, eternal life is given to us as a free gift. It cannot be earned.*)

10. What did Jesus ask the young man to do? (*To sell everything he had and give it to the poor.*)

11. What did Jesus say would be the result? (*He would receive treasure in Heaven; he would inherit eternal life.*)

12. How did the young man react? (*He became sad because he was a man of great wealth.*)

13. Jesus had said that the ruler lacked one thing. What do you think that was? (*He loved his money and his possessions more than he loved God.*)

14. Why did Jesus say it is hard for the rich to enter the kingdom of God? (*Riches may keep a person's interests and affections on material things and off of God.*)

15. Did Jesus mean that no rich people will enter Heaven? Explain. (*No, salvation is available for peo-*

ple of every economic status, but it may be harder for those who find every monetary need filled to place Jesus first in their lives.)

*16. Do you think that God expects us to sell all our personal possessions, leave our families, and follow Him? (*No, He seldom asks this of people.*)

*17. What is He asking of us? (*To love Him more than our personal possessions, to place Him first in our lives.*)

18. What did Jesus mean by, "'What is impossible with men is possible with God'"? (*No one in his own strength can put money and personal possessions in their proper perspective, only through the grace of God can we all be saved.*)

19. What was the young ruler's biggest problem and the result? (*He did not place Jesus first in his life; he walked away unsaved.*)

*20. Challenge: This coming week, find something in your life that has become a priority, but should not be. Ask God to help you place Him first in your life.

Activity 1: Priorities

Ask the students to list the five most important things in their lives in order of importance from one to five. Allow five minutes for them to do this. Then ask them to look at the list and see where they placed their relationship with Jesus. Have those who are willing to name the items on their lists. Ask the class to think about items which probably should not be on their lists and priorities which should be included on the papers.

Activity 2: Bible Pictionary

Divide the students into teams of three to five members. You must have an even number of teams. Have two teams sit at each table. Give each table the following words from recent lessons on slips of paper or recipe cards. First one team member draws a card and sketches it out on a piece of paper for his teammates. Allow two minutes for the team to guess the word. If they succeed, they get a point. Then the other team gets a turn, and one of their members chooses a card and sketches the picture. Continue until you run out of words or time. The team with the most points wins.

RULER	COMMANDMENTS	NEIGHBOR	ASLEEP
TREASURE	CAMEL	DISCIPLES	VILLAGE
NEEDLE	BLIND	DEAD	STONE
PARENTS	NIGHT	LISTEN	SPEAK

Thoughts for the Day

The leader should summarize the ideas presented in the following thoughts.

The young ruler wanted to inherit eternal life. Yet, he gave all his time, his thoughts, and his energy to his wealth. Jesus knew that the young man's attachment to his personal possessions placed a barrier between him and God. That is why Jesus asked him to sell everything and give the money to the poor. But the young ruler did not want to obey Jesus' command, and he walked away sad.

Jesus does not ask us to sell all our possessions, but He does ask us to love Him more than anyone or anything. To inherit everlasting life, we must place Him first in our lives.

Memory Verse

A copy of the memory verse should be made for each student to take home. After the leader distributes the copies, the class can say the verse aloud together.

"Jesus replied, 'What is impossible with men is possible with God'" (Luke 18:27).

Prayer

To conclude the session, the leader leads in prayer, allowing time for individual prayers by the students.

Dear God, help us not to place too much emphasis on our personal possessions. Teach us to surrender first place in our hearts and our lives to You. In Jesus' name, amen.

Next Week

The leader briefly mentions the next week's lesson, "Bartimaeus Receives His Sight" (Luke 18:35-43). Why was Bartimaeus shouting at Jesus? How did the people's attitude change? Next week we will study about a man who set an example of following Jesus and praising God.

Bartimaeus Receives His Sight

Scripture Text

Luke 18:35-43

Teacher's Tidbits

Jesus approached Jericho on His way to Jerusalem for the Passover. He taught the group of pilgrims around Him as He walked. Many villagers, who could not go to Jerusalem themselves, lined the wayside to watch the travelers pass.

The blind man named Bartimaeus sat among the onlooking crowd. He knew Jesus had healed many individuals and that people regarded Him as the possible Messiah. As Jesus approached, the blind beggar began to believe in Him as the Christ, so he called out, "'Jesus, Son of David.'"

The blind man's screams of utter desperation were so loud that the people around Jesus missed what He was saying. They told Bartimaeus to be quiet, but he would not be silenced. The man was determined to come face-to-face with Jesus.

The people who rebuked the beggar probably thought he desired money. His shouting appeared improper to them. Jesus showed the people that the man wanted his sight, not a handout.

Bartimaeus joined the caravan, and he glorified God by giving Him the honor, praise, and thanks for healing him. Many people witnessed the miracle.

What to Bring

Bibles, pencils, paper, a copy of Activity 1 for each student, and slips of paper or 3"-by-5" cards with the Bible personalities written on them from Activity 1.

Questions for Discussion

There may be more than one correct answer for each of the following questions. The leader will ask the questions and wait for the students to provide the answers. The leader should not supply an answer unless it is necessary.

1. Where was Jesus going? (*See verse 31. Jesus was on His way to Jerusalem for the Passover.*)

2. Why had a crowd gathered? (*Jesus attracted many pilgrims who were also traveling to Jerusalem, plus many lined the wayside to watch them pass.*)

3. Who did the crowd say was passing by? (*Jesus of Nazareth.*)

4. What was the blind beggar's name? (*Bartimaeus.*)

5. What did he call out? (*"Jesus, Son of David, have mercy on me."*)

6. Why did the man call Jesus "Son of David"? (*He had heard about the people Jesus had healed; he believed Him to be the Christ; he knew Jesus was related to King David.*)

7. Why did the people rebuke Bartimaeus? (*His shouting probably kept them from hearing Jesus' words; they probably thought he was asking for money.*)

8. Was the man easily silenced? What did he do? (*No! He shouted louder and refused to be silenced.*)

9. How would you describe Bartimaeus' personality? (*Persistent, bold, courageous, knew exactly what he wanted, passionate, determined to attract Jesus' attention.*)

*10. What do you think would be the greatest problem in being blind? (*Traveling because you could not drive or ride a bike, reading, and picturing the beautiful flowers, mountains, and so on.*)

*11. Do you know anyone who is blind? (*Allow time for those who do to tell about their friends or family members.*)

12. Why did Jesus question Bartimaeus? (*He wanted the crowd to know that the beggar desired his sight, not money.*)

13. What did Bartimaeus ask for? (*His sight; he wanted to see.*)

14. How did Jesus respond? (*"Receive your sight; your faith has healed you."*)

15. Jesus said, "'Your faith has healed you'" in a past lesson to whom? (*The bleeding woman who touched Jesus' cloak.*)

16. How is this story different from the blind man who was healed in lesson 14? (*The man in John was born blind; he did not ask to be healed; he was not healed instantly but went to the Pool of Siloam to receive his sight.*)

17. What did Bartimaeus do when he was healed

Hallelujah! Jesus just healed my eyes!

instantly? (*He followed Jesus and joined the pilgrimage to Jerusalem. He glorified God by giving Him the honor, praise, and thanks for healing him.*)

18. What effect did this have on the enormous crowd? (*When they saw it, they also praised God.*)

*19. What effect do our actions have on those who are standing around watching us? (*Our peers can be greatly influenced by our behavior; actions speak louder than words.*)

*20. Challenge: This coming week, make sure you are a good influence on your peers and that your actions are always pleasing to God.

Activity 1: Your Faith Has Healed You

Place an X next to all the people from past lessons who were healed or saved because of their own faith. Mark an O next to those someone else's faith healed. Leave those blank who walked away unhealed or unsaved.

NICODEMUS	SAMARITAN WOMAN
OFFICIAL'S SICK SON	PARALYTIC
MATTHEW	CENTURION'S SERVANT
JAIRUS' DAUGHTER	BLEEDING WOMAN
PETER	CANAANITE WOMAN'S DAUGHTER
MAN BORN BLIND	LAZARUS
RICH YOUNG MAN	BARTIMAEUS

Solution

X	NICODEMUS	X	SAMARITAN WOMAN
O	OFFICIAL'S SICK SON	O	PARALYTIC
X	MATTHEW	O	CENTURION'S SERVANT
O	JAIRUS' DAUGHTER	X	BLEEDING WOMAN
X	PETER	O	CANAANITE WOMAN'S DAUGHTER
X	MAN BORN BLIND	O	LAZARUS
O	RICH YOUNG MAN	X	BARTIMAEUS

Activity 2: Actions Speaks Louder Than Words

Give eight students slips of paper or 3"-by-5" cards with one of the following names on it. Have the students take turns acting out the following personalities, while the class tries to guess who they are. Allow two or three minutes for each charade. The students may make up their own names if preferred.

JOHN THE BAPTIST	CENTURION
BLIND MAN	SAMARITAN WOMAN
NICODEMUS	MATTHEW
PETER	MARTHA

Thoughts for the Day

The leader should summarize the ideas presented in the following thoughts.

Bartimaeus persistently followed Jesus, begging to have his sight restored. He believed that Jesus was the Christ and he called out, "'Jesus, Son of David.'"

When he received his sight, Bartimaeus joined the pilgrimage and followed Jesus to Jerusalem. He praised God for the gift of sight. The crowd, following his example, praised God, too.

Because we are Christians, others closely watch our actions.

Memory Verse

A copy of the memory verse should be made for each student to take home. After the leader distributes the copies, the class can say the verse aloud together.

"And they praised God because of me" (Galatians 1:24).

Prayer

To conclude the session, the leader leads in prayer, allowing time for individual prayers by the students.

Dear God, thank You for listening to the desires of our hearts. Please help us to be good role models. In Jesus' name, amen.

Next Week

The leader briefly mentions the next week's lesson, "Zacchaeus Is Converted" (Luke 19:1-10). Next week we will study about a wealthy tax collector who found an unusual way of getting Jesus' attention.

Zacchaeus Is Converted

Scripture Text

Luke 19:1-10

Teacher's Tidbits

The leader should read this section at home before the day of the lesson.

In Biblical times Jericho was a wealthy and important town on the main road between Jerusalem and the east. Jericho afforded excellent opportunities for dishonesty, because it was one of the greatest taxation centers in ancient Palestine.

Zacchaeus was an Israelite tax collector who was lonely, despised, and hated by men. His riches probably had not all been obtained in an honest way, but Zacchaeus changed. His name is Hebrew for righteous. Ultimately, he volunteered to give half his money to the poor, and he promised to restore fourfold anything taken fraudulently. This was more than the law demanded for voluntary restitution.

The tree Zacchaeus climbed was a sycamore-fig tree with leaves like a mulberry tree and fruit like figs. The tree was easy to climb with its short trunk and wide lateral branches forking out in all directions.

Jesus came to save those who were lost. Lost means in the wrong place. A person is lost when he has wandered away from God or has never known God. He is found when he accepts Jesus as his Savior and takes his rightful place in the family of God.

What to Bring

Bibles, pencils, paper, four pieces of candy, gum, or another inexpensive item for each student for Activity 1, the items on the lost and found list from Activity 2 to be hidden before the students arrive, and a copy of the lost items from Activity 2 for each student.

Questions for Discussion

There may be more than one correct answer for each of the following questions. The leader will ask the questions and wait for the students to provide the answers. The leader should not supply an answer unless it is necessary.

1. What do you know about Jericho? (*It was a trade center between Jerusalem and the east; it was the city conquered by Joshua.*)

2. What do you know about Zacchaeus? (*He was a chief tax collector; he was short and wealthy.*)

3. How do you think the people of Jericho felt about Zacchaeus? (*He was probably despised since he was a tax collector.*)

4. Why couldn't he see Jesus? (*The crowd probably would not let him through, plus he was too short to see over the crowd.*)

5. Do you think he intended to speak to Jesus? (*No, he probably just wanted to see Him.*)

6. Why was he so anxious to see Jesus that he climbed a tree? (*He was curious; perhaps he had heard that Jesus did not reject tax collectors.*)

7. Why did Jesus want to stay at Zacchaeus' house? (*Jesus knew this man could be saved.*)

8. How did Zacchaeus react to Jesus' request? (*He came down from the tree immediately and welcomed Jesus.*)

9. How did this contrast with the reaction of the people? (*They complained that Jesus had gone to be the guest of a sinner; they considered themselves better than Zacchaeus.*)

10. What did Zacchaeus offer to do? (*To give half of his possessions to the poor, and to pay back four times the amount that he had cheated people.*)

11. What does this say about his past behavior in tax collecting? (*He probably cheated people.*)

12. How do you feel about his compensation of offering four times the amount? (*Jesus had a tremendous impact on him; he became generous; the amount was greater than the law demanded for voluntary restitution.*)

13. What did Jesus say to Zacchaeus? (*"Today, salvation has come to this house."*)

14. What change took place in Zacchaeus? (*He was repentant; he was willing to take action to back up his words; he became joyful because he knew Jesus had pardoned him for the wrong things he had done.*)

*15. Do our words mean anything if they are not backed up by action? Explain. (*No, people watch how we live our lives; they watch our actions closely to see if our behavior matches our words or what we should do.*)

*16. How can we live out what we say we will do in our actions? (*Allow time for as many students as have ideas to speak on this important subject.*)

17. How would you compare and contrast Zacchaeus with Matthew? (*Both immediately came when Jesus called; both found salvation, both showed changed lives; Matthew gave up tax collecting while Zacchaeus paid back four times the amount he had extorted.*)

*18. What was Jesus' mission on earth according to this passage? (*To seek out the lost and to rescue them, the conversion of sinners.*)

*19. What should we do if we have wronged someone? (*Allow time for several students to share their views on this important question. Find a way to say we are sorry or to right the wrong with that individual.*)

*20. Challenge: Think of a time when you have wronged someone. Either speak to the person or write the individual a note and apologize.

Activity 1: Fourfold Repayment

Hand out a piece of candy, gum, or another inexpensive item to each student. Tell them not to eat it. Wait a minute or two, and then tell the students you are collecting taxes from them. They must pay with the item that was given to them.

Wait until after the second activity has been completed. Then give each young person four times as much candy, gum, or whatever was originally given to them. This is what Zacchaeus did when he paid back four times the amount he had stolen.

Activity 2: Lost and Found

Before the students arrive, hide the following items in a large room or several rooms. Give each student a list of the items. Allow fifteen minutes, or until one person has found all the items.

HAIR CLIP	BUTTON
SAFETY PIN	ORANGE MARKING PEN
STICK OF GUM	PAPER BAG
PIECE OF YARN	COFFEE MUG
FORK	CANDY BAR

Do not forget to hand out four times the amount of the item in Activity 1 that you took from each student, and explain what you are doing.

Thoughts for the Day

The leader should summarize the ideas presented in the following thoughts.

Zacchaeus climbed a tree to see Jesus, although he had no intention of meeting him. But Jesus knew that Zacchaeus was lost. He also realized that Zacchaeus was willing to repent and be saved, so He asked to stay at the tax collector's home.

Zacchaeus realized his selfish attitude toward his possessions, and he confessed that it was wrong to charge more than the lawful amount in taxes. He wished to change his actions now that Jesus was part of his life.

When Jesus becomes part of our lives a change takes place, too. Other people can see this change by our actions more than by our words.

Memory Verse

A copy of the memory verse should be made for each student to take home. After the leader distributes the copies, the class can say the verse aloud together.

"'For the Son of Man came to seek and to save what was lost'" (Luke 19:10).

Prayer

To conclude the session, the leader leads in prayer, allowing time for individual prayers by the students.

Dear Lord, thank You for coming to earth to save those who are lost. If we have wronged people, help us to make things right again. Teach us to show others that we belong to You by our actions and our words. In Jesus' name, amen.

Next Week

The leader briefly mentions the next week's lesson, "Lazarus Is Raised From the Dead" (John 11:1-44). Why did Jesus wait two days to leave for Bethany when He knew Lazarus was sick? What important secret did Jesus share with Martha when He arrived? Next week we will study how Lazarus walked out of the tomb after being dead for four days.

Lazarus Is Raised From the Dead

Scripture Text

John 11:1-44

Teacher's Tidbits

The leader should read this section at home before the day of the lesson.

In Biblical times everyone who was capable joined the funeral procession. Curiously enough, the women walked first because Eve's first sin brought death into the world. No food was prepared in the house of the deceased. Deep mourning lasted for seven days. Respect for the dead and sympathy for the mourners were essential parts of Jewish duty.

The typical Palestinian tomb was a natural cave. It contained a six-by-nine-foot chamber with eight shelves cut in the rock on which the bodies were lain. Each body was wrapped in linen, while the hands and feet were swathed in bandage-like wrappings, and the head was covered separately. The tomb had no door, but a stone was rolled across the entrance to seal it. This tomb was probably similar to the one in which Jesus was placed on Good Friday.

The Jewish working day was divided into twelve equal hours from sunrise to sunset. The length of the hours varied according to the length of the day and the season of the year. Today the length of our hours is standard, but there is still enough time in every day for each person to do what God wants him to do.

Perhaps Jesus waited two days before going to Bethany because He wanted the action to be on His own initiative, not on the persuasion of anyone else. Often we want Jesus to do things our way, in our timing. Yet, we must allow Him to do them in His own way, on His time schedule.

What to Bring

Bibles, pencils, paper, and a copy of the questions from Activity 2 for each small group.

Questions for Discussion

There may be more than one correct answer for each of the following questions. The leader will ask the questions and wait for the students to provide the answers. The leader should not supply an answer unless it is necessary.

1. What was the message that Mary and Martha sent to Jesus? (*"Lord, the one you love is sick."*)

2. Why didn't the women ask Jesus to come? (*They felt their statement of need would bring Him immediately.*)

3. What purpose did He give for Lazarus' sickness? (*Not to end in death, but to glorify God.*)

4. Did Jesus go immediately to His dear friends in Bethany? (*No, He waited two days.*)

5. Why do you think He waited so long? (*He wanted the action to be on His own initiative, not on anyone else's.*)

*6. Do you often want things to happen on your time schedule? Explain. (*Allow time for several students to share their ideas.*)

*7. Has anything special happened to you when you waited for God's timing? (*Allow time for as many students as are willing to speak on this exciting topic.*)

8. Why did the disciples want Jesus to stay out of Judea? (*The Jews tried to stone Him there; the Pharisees were plotting against Him.*)

9. What did Jesus mean by twelve hours of daylight? (*The Jewish working day was divided into twelve equal hours from daylight to sunset; they worked during the daylight hours.*)

10. What was Thomas' attitude about going to Bethany? (*He was ready to die with Jesus.*)

11. How long had Lazarus been dead when Jesus arrived? (*Four days.*)

12. What did Martha say when she greeted Jesus? (*"I know that even now God will give you whatever you ask."*)

13. What does this show about Martha? (*She had great faith and understanding in Jesus.*)

14. What was Jesus' response to her? (*"I am the resurrection and the life. He who believes in Me will live."*)

*15. What do verses 25, 26 mean to you? (*Believers, being united to Jesus in faith, will share His risen life even though we will experience bodily death.*)

16. What different names did Martha call Jesus?

(*Lord; Christ; Son of God; and the Teacher.*)

17. Why did Jesus cry? (*He identified with a family He loved; He showed He was human.*)

18. Why did Jesus pray the way He did instead of asking that Lazarus be raised from the dead? (*He prayed aloud for the benefit of the many bystanders; He already knew that Lazarus would be raised from the dead.*)

19. How did Lazarus walking from the grave differ from Jesus when He ascended? (*Lazarus was tangled in his grave clothes; Jesus left the grave clothes behind.*)

*20. Challenge: Think about what you want people to remember about you after you have left this earth and gone to Heaven.

Activity 1: Legacy

Someday each of us will die unless the Lord returns first. What would you like people to remember about you after you have left this earth and gone to Heaven?

Allow five minutes for the students to write down one thing they would like to have people remember about them. Then have those students who are willing share their ideas. Do not force anyone to speak on this sensitive topic.

Activity 2: Jesus Always Answers

Divide the class into small groups of three to five students. Ask each group to choose a leader. Allow them ten minutes to discuss the following questions. Then reconvene the class. Ask the leaders to share their group's answers.

1. Does Jesus always answer our prayers? (*Yes, He always promises to respond when we ask Him for something.*)

2. What are some of His answers? (*Yes; no; wait a while.*)

3. What did we learn about answers to prayer from the lesson? (*Sometimes we need to wait for God's timing; sometimes the answers are better than we ever imagined; Jesus waited four days to answer Mary and Martha.*)

4. How has God answered your prayers lately?

Thoughts for the Day

The leader should summarize the ideas presented in the following thoughts.

Lazarus was a special friend of Jesus. Yet, Jesus waited until he had been dead four days to raise him to life again. It is weird to think of the bandaged Lazarus staggering from the tomb. Sometimes Jesus' timing is not our timing, but what He has in mind for us can be infinitely more wonderful than we ever imagined.

Jesus is the resurrection and the life. If we have faith that He is the Son of God who forgives our sins, then we will share His everlasting life.

Memory Verse

A copy of the memory verse should be made for each student to take home. After the leader distributes the copies, the class can say the verse aloud together.

"'I am the resurrection and the life. He who believes in me will live, even though he dies; and whoever lives and believes in me will never die. Do you believe this'" (John 11:25, 26)?

Prayer

To conclude the session, the leader leads in prayer, allowing time for individual prayers by the students.

Dear Lord, teach us to wait for Your timing in the answers to our prayers. Thank You for giving us everlasting life. In Jesus' name, amen.

Next Week

The leader briefly mentions the next week's lesson, "Mary Anoints Jesus With Perfume" (John 12:1-11). Why did Mary pour perfume on Jesus' feet? Who objected to this action and why? Next week we will study about a special act of love Mary showed toward Jesus.

Mary Annoints Jesus With Perfume

Scripture Text

John 12:1-11

Teacher's Tidbits

In Biblical times Passover was one of the three Pilgrimage Festivals to Jerusalem made by every male Jew who was physically able to travel. Matzoh, unleavened bread, is eaten during the holiday. This bread serves as a constant reminder of the poverty suffered by the Israelites in Egyptian bondage. When the Israelites abandoned Egypt, they did not have time to wait for their bread to rise.

Oil was normally poured on the head. It was unusual that Mary poured it on Jesus' feet—an act showing humility, love, and devotion. The expensive perfume was worth a year's wages for the laborer, three hundred denarii. Unbinding of the hair was a sign of deepest grief, and a Jewish woman never let down her hair in public. Washing the feet was equivalent to a complete bath.

We see Mary's act as the symbolic embalming of Jesus' body for burial as though He were already dead. The house was filled with fragrance, representing the time when the gospel would eventually fill the world.

What to Bring

Bibles, pencils, paper, a bottle opener and a bottle of pop for each relay team for Activity 2, and a copy of Activity 1 for each student.

Questions for Discussion

There may be more than one correct answer for each of the following questions. The leader will ask the questions and wait for the students to provide the answers. The leader should not supply an answer unless it is necessary.

1. When did Jesus arrive in Bethany? (*Six days before the Passover.*)

2. What happened before in Bethany? (*Jesus visited with Mary and Martha and raised Lazarus from the dead.*)

3. What was Martha doing? Does this fit with her personality in the past? (*She served the meal as she did in Lesson 15.*)

4. How did people eat differently in Biblical times than they do today? (*They reclined on couches around the table.*)

5. Why did Mary pour the perfume on Jesus' feet? (*As an act of humility, love, and devotion. It was symbolic of embalming His body for burial.*)

6. How much do you think the perfume cost? (*Three hundred denarii, a year's wages for a laborer.*)

*7. Do you think Mary should have spent this much money and poured it on Jesus' feet? Should the money have been given to the poor? Explain. (*Allow as much time as is available to debate this interesting issue.*)

*8. Does this mean we should not give money to the poor? Explain. (*No, in this case Mary showed that devotion to Jesus takes precedence over giving to those in need. Jesus wants us to give to others; He wants us to place Him first in our lives.*)

*9. To what could you compare the house being filled with the fragrance? (*To the time when the gospel would fill the world.*)

10. Why did Judas object to the purchase of the perfume? (*He kept the money bag for the disciples and stole from it.*)

11. What characteristics do you note in Jesus' answer to Judas? (*He shows authority and a definite opinion, perhaps anger.*)

12. What did Judas ultimately do? (*He betrayed Jesus for thirty silver coins, threw the money into the temple, and hanged himself.*)

13. What does Jesus mean by saying that Mary should save the perfume for the day of His burial? (*Her act of love was symbolic of preparing His body for burial. Jesus was on His way to Jerusalem to die on the cross, and because He died on the Sabbath, there was no time to prepare His body for burial.*)

14. Why does Jesus say, "'You will always have the poor among you, but you will not always have me'"? (*He realized that He was on the way to His death, and Jesus wanted His followers to be prepared for* *that difficult time.)*

15. Why had such a large crowd gathered? (*To see Lazarus, whom Jesus had raised from the dead, as well as to see Jesus.*)

16. How is hostility shown by the high priests and Pharisees? (*They made plans to kill Lazarus as well as Jesus.*)

17. What motive did these religious Jewish leaders have for their violence? (*Because of Lazarus' testimony, many of the Jews were putting their faith in Jesus.*)

18. Would Mary have had a later opportunity to show her love and devotion toward Jesus in this way? (*No, she probably never saw Him again after He left for Jerusalem until His resurrection.*)

*19. Why should we be reminded to do special things for others and for our Lord now? (*We may not get another opportunity.*)

*20. Challenge: Do something special for a friend or family member this coming week.

Activity 1: Light and Shadow

The presence of Jesus and Mary's love represent light. Judas' selfish resentment represents shadow. Place an L for light or an S for shadow in front of the following people from past and future lessons.

JOHN THE BAPTIST	THE DEVIL
NATHANAEL	NICODEMUS
PHARISEES	SCRIBES
THE SAMARITAN WOMAN	MATTHEW
THE CENTURION	BARTIMAEUS
LAZARUS	MARTHA
RICH YOUNG RULER	ZACCHAEUS
PILATE	HEROD

Solution

L	JOHN THE BAPTIST	S	THE DEVIL
L	NATHANAEL	L	NICODEMUS
S	PHARISEES	S	SCRIBES
L	THE SAMARITAN WOMAN	L	MATTHEW
L	THE CENTURION	L	BARTIMAEUS
L	LAZARUS	L	MARTHA
S	RICH YOUNG RULER	L	ZACCHAEUS
S	PILATE	S	HEROD

Activity 2: Soda-Pop Relay

Divide the group into teams of six to eight players. Give the first person in each line a bottle opener. Place a bottle of pop out in front of each team some distance away. Each person on the team has to run around the bottle of pop and run back to hand the bottle opener to the next member of the team. When the bottle opener gets back to the first member of the team again, that student runs out to the bottle of pop, opens it, and drinks it. The first team whose leader drinks the pop wins.

Thoughts for the Day

The leader should summarize the ideas presented in the following thoughts.

In an act of humility and love, Mary poured expensive perfume on the feet of Jesus. This was a symbol of anointing His body for burial, for soon He would die on the cross.

Showing devotion for Jesus is an important expression of being a Christian. Mary seized her opportunity while Jesus was with her. Let's remember to do thoughtful things for others now, for the chance may never come again.

Memory Verse

A copy of the memory verse should be made for each student to take home. After the leader distributes the copies, the class can say the verse.

"'Be wise in the way you act toward outsiders; make the most of every opportunity'" (Colossians 4:5).

Prayer

To conclude the session, the leader leads in prayer.

Dear Lord, teach us to show our love and devotion to You. In Jesus' name, amen.

Next Week

The leader briefly mentions the next week's lesson, "Peter Denies Jesus Three Times" (Luke 22:31-34, 54-62). Next week we will study about a dramatic scene that ultimately strengthened Peter's faith.

Peter Denies Jesus Three Times

Scripture Text

Luke 22:31-34, 54-62

Teacher's Tidbits

Shortly after midnight the soldiers brought Jesus to the palace of the high priest. Peter followed at a distance. John knew the high priest, so he went into the courtyard, but Peter was stopped at the gate. John went back, spoke to the girl, and asked her to let Peter in.

When Peter spoke, his guttural pronunciation revealed that he was a Galilean. By denying his identity, Peter denied his Lord, also. Peter's trial formed an ironic sub-plot to the trial of Jesus.

When the rooster crowed, Jesus looked at Peter with sorrow and deep affection, piercing his heart like a sword. The penalty for Peter was to face the heartbreak in Jesus' eyes. Peter realized he had acted like a coward. His tears were a mark of true repentance and a turning point in his life. This scene took place the evening before Christ's crucifixion.

What to Bring

Bibles, pencils, slips of paper, a towel used as a turban for Activity 2, and a time line from Activity 1 for each student.

Questions for Discussion

There may be more than one correct answer for each of the following questions. The leader will ask the questions and wait for the students to provide the answers. The leader should not supply an answer unless it is necessary.

1. Why did Jesus call Peter by his former name Simon? (*Peter means rock, and Jesus reminded Peter of his human weakness.*)

2. What was Satan trying to do? (*Satan made a last, desperate attempt to break up the circle of Jesus' disciples and scatter them as he had done to Judas.*)

3. How did Jesus handle Satan's attempt? (*Jesus said a special prayer for Peter and the other disciples; He prayed that their faith would not fail.*)

4. What did Jesus challenge Peter to do? (*When his faith was strong again, he could encourage others and help them to become strong.*)

5. What was Peter's reply? (*"Lord, I am ready to go with You to prison and to death."*)

6. What did Jesus predict? (*That Peter would deny Him three times that day before the rooster crowed.*)

7. Where did they take Jesus? (*To the house of the high priest.*)

8. How did Peter react? (*He followed at a distance, but he did not abandon his Lord.*)

9. How did they know Peter was with Jesus? (*Perhaps they had seen Peter with Jesus; they recognized the guttural pronunciation of the Galilean accent.*)

10. Why did Peter deny being with Jesus? (*He feared for his life; he lost his self-confidence.*)

*11. Have you ever been afraid to admit you were a Christian? Explain. (*Allow time for several students to tell about their experiences.*)

*12. Have you told a lie because you were afraid of the consequences? Explain. (*Do not force anyone who is not willing to share on this sensitive subject. Have everyone think about the answer silently.*)

13. What did Peter say in his denials? (*"Woman, I don't know him.'" "'Man, I am not!'" "'Man, I don't know what you're talking about.'"*)

14. What happened while Peter spoke his third denial? (*The rooster crowed, and Jesus turned and looked at Peter.*)

15. With what kind of facial expression did Jesus look at Peter? (*With a mixture of sorrow and deep affection.*)

16. How did this affect Peter? (*He remembered what Jesus had predicted earlier; remorse struck him and he wept; he knew he had failed.*)

17. What change do you think took place in Peter? (*He repented, and later he became the leader of the disciples and strengthened them.*)

18. How did Peter use this failure to encourage the other disciples? (*Because he experienced the shame of failure, he realized that all of the disciples would face obstacles, and he could help the others.*)

*19. Have you ever experienced a feeling of failure

like Peter did? Explain. (*Allow time for those students who are willing to share.*)

*20. Challenge: Pray that you may overcome any feelings of failure that you may have in your heart.

Activity 1: Time Line of People Who Met Jesus

Put the following incidents regarding people who met Jesus in the order they occurred. This may be done individually or in teams of three to five players.

Matthew is called to be a disciple.
The paralytic can walk.
Zacchaeus is converted.
Lazarus is raised from the dead.
Nicodemus hears about a new birth.
Peter walks on water.
Mary anoints Jesus with perfume.
The Samaritan woman learns about living water.
John the Baptist baptizes Jesus.
The Devil tempts Jesus.

Solution

John the Baptist baptizes Jesus.
The Devil tempts Jesus.
Nicodemus hears about a new birth.
The Samaritan woman learns about living water.
The paralytic can walk.
Matthew is called to be a disciple.
Peter walks on water.
Zacchaeus is converted.
Lazarus is raised from the dead.
Mary anoints Jesus with perfume.

Activity 2: Manny the Magnificent

Give everyone a slip of paper and ask them to write a short sentence on it. The slips are folded and put in a container for Manny. Manny wears a turban on his head. He can be a leader or an outgoing student. He places his own slip in the container with a special mark on it so he can save it until last.

Manny announces that he will read the slips of paper without opening them. He picks one of the papers, rubs it on his forehead, and makes up something that might have been written on the paper. He looks at the paper and discovers he is wrong. He picks up the second paper, rubs it on his forehead, and repeats the sentence written on the first paper. He opens the second paper and confirms that he is correct. Then he asks the person who wrote the sentence to identify it. Everyone is impressed.

Having seen what was on the second paper, he reads that after he rubs the third paper on his forehead. Each time he opens the paper to see if he is

correct, he is actually learning the next sentence. He saves his own slip until last, and reads what was on the previous paper. If done correctly, this will really baffle the group.

Thoughts for the Day

The leader should summarize the ideas presented in the following thoughts.

Peter said he was willing to go to prison or die with Jesus. Yet, when he became frightened, he denied knowing Jesus three times. Jesus knew that Peter would struggle and fail, but He prayed that Peter's faith would be strengthened through the crisis.

Peter realized he had acted like a coward. In time, he encouraged many people. Let us learn to encourage our friends and family members like Peter did.

Memory Verse

A copy of the memory verse should be made for each student to take home.

"'But I have prayed for you, Simon, that your faith may not fail. And when you have turned back, strengthen your brothers'" (Luke 22:32).

Prayer

To conclude the session, the leader leads in prayer.

Dear Lord, please strengthen us when we become frightened that our faith may not fail. In Jesus' name, amen.

Next Week

The leader briefly mentions the next week's lesson, "Pilate Questions Jesus" (Luke 23:1-25). Next week we will study about the charges brought against Jesus.

Pilate Questions Jesus

Scripture Text

Luke 23:1-25

Teacher's Tidbits

The leader should read this section at home before the day of the lesson.

Because the Jews did not possess the power of capital punishment, they went to the Roman officials to seek the death penalty for Jesus. The Jewish tribunal, the Sanhedrin, charged Jesus with blasphemy because He dared to call Himself the Son of God. Before Pilate, these charges were never mentioned because they carried no weight with him.

The Jewish religious leaders instigated the crucifixion of Jesus. They feared He would cause them to lose their wealth, comfort, and power. They charged Jesus with inciting the people, with encouraging men not to pay taxes to Caesar, and with assuming the title of King.

Pilate was an experienced Roman official who saw through their plans. He had no desire to gratify their wishes, but he didn't want to offend them either.

When they mentioned He was from notorious Galilee to add fuel to the accusations, Pilate found a way out. But Herod's return of Jesus implied His innocence.

Pilate did not want to condemn Jesus. He told the Jews to settle the matter themselves. He whipped Jesus and tried to release Him at Passover. But the Jews compelled Pilate to condemn Jesus by holding the threat of an official report to Rome over his head. He sentenced Jesus to death in order to remain governor of Palestine.

What to Bring

Bibles, pencils, paper, a copy of the crossword puzzle from page 51 for each student, and seven copies of the skit from Activity 2.

Questions for Discussion

There may be more than one correct answer for each of the following questions. The leader will ask the questions and wait for the students to provide the answers. The leader should not supply an answer unless it is necessary.

1. Who was the assembly mentioned in verse 1? (*The Sanhedrin, the Jewish council of priests and elders presided over by the high priest.*)

2. What charge did the Sanhedrin bring against Jesus? (*Blasphemy, because He had called Himself the Son of God.*)

3. Why did they take Jesus before Pilate to be tried again? (*They wanted the death penalty, and they did not have the power to issue it, only Rome could sentence a man to death.*)

4. What charges against Jesus were brought before Pilate? (*Inciting the people, encouraging men not to pay taxes to Caesar, and assuming the title of king.*)

5. Why did they not accuse Him of blasphemy as the Sanhedrin had charged? (*This would not carry any weight with Pilate.*)

6. Did Pilate think Jesus was guilty? Explain. (*No, he found no basis for a charge against Jesus.*)

7. How did Pilate try to escape sentencing Jesus? (*When he found out Jesus was a Galilean and under Herod's jurisdiction, he sent Jesus to Herod.*)

8. How did Herod react to Jesus at first? (*He asked many questions; he regarded Jesus as a spectacle.*)

9. How did Jesus respond to Herod? (*By total silence.*)

10. Why didn't Jesus answer Herod? (*Herod had ordered the beheading of John the Baptist; Jesus knew that Herod had no respect for Him.*)

11. Why did Herod ridicule and mock Jesus? (*He was offended at Jesus' unwillingness to answer questions; he took revenge.*)

12. Do you think Herod believed Jesus was guilty? Explain. (*No, he would have tried Jesus if he had a case; his return of Jesus implied innocence.*)

13. What happened between Pilate and Herod as a result of this incident? (*They became friends.*)

14. What was Pilate's next solution? (*He said Jesus had done nothing that deserved death, so he offered to punish Him and release Him.*)

15. How did the Jews respond? (*Release Barabbas! Crucify Jesus!*)

16. Why did Pilate ultimately give in to the Jews? (*He* *was afraid they would complain to Rome about the job he was doing.)*

*17. Who do you hold most responsible for the death of Jesus? (*Allow several students to express their opinions.*)

*18. Can you think of an example today when someone was wrongly accused? (*Allow time for as many students as are willing to share on this subject.*)

*19. How can you personally stop this from happening? (*Allow several students to speak. By not repeating gossip; by not listening to gossip.*)

*20. Challenge: This coming week, make sure you do not listen to or repeat any gossip.

Activity 1: Crossword: People Who Met Jesus

Give each student a copy of the puzzle on page 51. Have them fill in the blanks with the appropriate person who met Jesus. (*Puzzle solution found on page 52.*)

Activity 2: The Mock Trial

Choose a judge, a defendant who is a good sport, a lawyer, several witnesses, and a jury.

Judge: The charges against the defendant are that she was seen taking money out of one of the lockers in the gym. We will try the case fairly and squarely to see if she is guilty or innocent.

Lawyer: You were seen with your hand in a locker when everyone else was outside. Is that true?

Defendant: Yes, I went into the locker room to take my cough medicine.

Lawyer: No one is allowed in the locker room during class.

I feel the defendant has already admitted her guilt.

(*Witness 1 takes the stand.*)

Witness 1: I went into the locker room during gym class and saw the defendant with her hand in a locker. I think it was Witness 2's locker.

Lawyer: There you have it. An eyewitness to the fact that the defendant was in the locker room when she should not have been and had her hand in a locker.

(*Witness 2 takes the stand.*)

Witness 2: When I went to lunch, I discovered that I had no money in my wallet. I think, no—I'm sure my mother gave me ten dollars this morning for my lunches this week. At least, she always does on Mondays.

Lawyer: You had ten dollars when you got to school, and after the defendant got into your locker, it was gone. Is that right?

Witness 2: Yes, I guess that must be the way it happened if you say so. And particularly if Witness 1 saw the defendant in my locker.

Lawyer: You see, jury, the defendant is guilty without a doubt. She should be suspended from school for stealing ten dollars and being in the locker room at an unauthorized time.

Judge: How do you plead?

Defendant: (*The defendant takes the stand again.*) Not guilty.

Judge: Jury, what is your verdict?

Jury: Guilty. Three against one, so she must be guilty.

Defendant: Guilty of taking cough medicine?

Judge: Justice has been served. (*Everyone cheers.*)

If time permits, discuss all the inconsistencies and unfair practices of this mock trial.

Thoughts for the Day

The leader should summarize the ideas presented in the following thoughts.

Because the Jewish religious officials wanted the death penalty for Jesus, they brought Him before Pilate and made up political charges.

Pilate did not want to condemn Jesus, and he tried four times to avoid passing sentence. Yet, in the end, he gave in to their demands.

Today, we hear gossip about our friends that is not true. Sometimes it is hard to know what to believe. We need to investigate the facts.

Memory Verse

A copy of the memory verse should be made for each student to take home.

"'Don't let anyone look down on you because you are young, but set an example for the believers in speech, in life, in love, in faith and in purity'" (1 Timothy 4:12).

Prayer

To conclude the session, the leader leads in prayer, allowing time for individual prayers by the students.

Dear Lord, help us not to listen to or to spread gossip. In Jesus' name, amen.

Next Week

The leader briefly mentions the next week's lesson, "The Repentant Criminal Asks to Be Remembered" (Luke 23:32-43). Next week we will study about a promise Jesus made just before His death on the cross.

People Who Met Jesus

Across:
4. Responded to Jesus' call
7. Poured perfume on Jesus
9. Blind beggar

Down:
1. Walked on water
2. Raised from the dead
3. Climbed a tree
4. Wanted new birth
5. Mary's sister
6. Servant was healed
8. Was a tax collector

Solution

```
          ¹P
           E
                  ²L        ³Z
  ⁴N  A  T  H  A  N  A  N  A  E  L
   I      E     Z        C
   C      R     A        C
   O            R        H
   D      ⁵M    U        A
   E      A     S        E          ⁶C
  ⁷M  A  R  Y            U          E
   U      T        ⁸M    S          N
   S      H        A                T
        ⁹B  A  R  T  I  M  A  E  U  S
           T                R
           H                I
           E                O
           W                N
```

The Repentant Criminal Asks to Be Remembered

Scripture Text

Luke 23:32-43

Teacher's Tidbits

The punishment of crucifixion on the cross was considered so terrible that Rome inflicted it only on slaves. No Roman citizen was crucified. The condemned person was bound to the cross with ropes, his arms and legs jerked out of joint, then nails were driven through the hands and feet. Half way up the cross a projecting piece of wood called the saddle took the weight of the criminal, for otherwise the nails would have torn through his hands.

The indescribable pain and disgrace were overwhelming. Soon fever racked the body, every nerve was aroused, and intense thirst set in. The wounds, not severe enough to cause a quick death but sufficient to cause extreme torture, became progressively intolerable. Finally, the man died from exhaustion, exposure, and loss of blood. Although crucifixion was the most agonizing and shameful form of execution ever devised, the spiritual suffering Jesus experienced of bearing all our sins was far greater.

Every Jew wore five articles of clothing—the inner tunic, the outer robe, the girdle, the sandals, and the turban. Jesus' outer robe was woven in one piece without a seam. To have cut it up would have ruined it, so the soldiers gambled for His robe in the shadow of the cross.

By answering the robber's prayer, Jesus shows us that it is never too late to turn to Him. While a person is alive, there is hope. Those who pray shall be rewarded, those who repent shall be forgiven. Whoever comes to Him shall receive everlasting life.

What to Bring

Bibles, pencils, paper, a copy of the hidden names of Jesus from Activity 2 for each student, and a balloon for each student.

Questions for Discussion

There may be more than one correct answer for each of the following questions. The leader will ask the questions and wait for the students to provide the answers. The leader should not supply an answer unless it is necessary.

1. Why do you think the authorities crucified Jesus between two known criminals? (*To humiliate Him and to associate Him with robbers.*)

2. Why do you think Jesus was placed in the middle? (*Because He was well-known, and the authorities wanted His death to be highly visible.*)

3. How did Jesus react to what they were doing? (*He asked God to forgive them. He held no resentment, no anger, no desire to punish the men who were mistreating Him.*)

4. What did Jesus want for those who crucified Him? (*He wanted them to have a second chance to repent before judgment was executed on them.*)

*5. What lesson today can we learn from Jesus' reaction to those who crucified Him? (*When people mistreat us, we must forgive as He forgave.*)

*6. Would you be willing to tell about a time when you had trouble forgiving someone? (*Do not force anyone who is not willing to answer on this sensitive subject. Everyone should think about this question silently.*)

*7. What happens inside of us when we refuse to forgive someone? (*Anger and bitterness fester within us and can affect our health and our outlook on life.*)

*8. What happens when we are able to forgive someone in our hearts? (*We feel a sense of peace and contentment; relationships are restored.*)

9. How did the rulers, soldiers, and people react to Jesus? (*They sneered and mocked Him.*)

10. Do you know what group of people were crucified in Biblical times? (*Only slaves, Roman citizens were never crucified.*)

11. How quickly do you think death came by crucifixion? (*Very slowly, the torture lasted hours, days, or sometimes weeks.*)

12. How painful was crucifixion? (*It was the most agonizing and shameful form of execution ever devised.*)

13. Why did Jesus refuse the wine vinegar offered by the soldiers to ease the pain? (*Jesus wanted to*

remain conscious and keep His mind clear throughout His suffering and death.)

14. What was even more painful for Jesus than suffering on the cross? (*The spiritual suffering of bearing all our sins was greater.*)

15. How did the criminals hanging next to Jesus react differently? (*One hurled insults at Jesus, while the other said, "'We are punished justly, . . . but this man has done nothing wrong . . . Jesus, remember me when you come into your kingdom.'"*)

16. What did Jesus promise him? (*"'Today you will be with me in paradise.'"*)

17. What does this promise show about the power of Jesus on the cross? (*Even though He felt weak hanging on the cross, He still possessed the power to distribute life or death.*)

*18. What lesson do you learn from this story? (*It is never too late to turn to Christ.*)

*19. What does the crucifixion of Jesus mean to you? (*Salvation, everlasting life in Heaven with Him.*)

*20. Challenge: This coming week, pray that God will help you to forgive someone who has hurt you in some way.

Activity 1: Race to Calvary

Divide the group into teams and give each person a deflated balloon. On a signal, the first member of each team blows up the balloon and lets it go.

The students run to where their balloon landed, blow it up again, and let it go. The object is to get the balloon across the goal line fifteen feet away.

When the first person reaches the goal line, he runs back and tags the next person on the team. Each team member does the same thing. The first team to have its last member cross the finish line wins.

Activity 2: Hidden Names of Jesus

After they hung Jesus on the cross, they placed a notice over Him that read: The King of the Jews. Twenty-five other names or descriptions of Jesus are scrambled below. The more difficult ones have an * for extra credit. The students may work individually or in small groups using pencils and sheets of paper to unscramble the names of Jesus.

	Solution
1. CENIPR FO CEEAP	PRINCE OF PEACE
2. DREPSHEH	SHEPHERD
3. SHEMSIA	MESSIAH
4. RHUTT	TRUTH
5. THILG FO HET DROWL	LIGHT OF THE WORLD
6. NECHOS NOE	CHOSEN ONE
7. THOREPP	PROPHET
8. LOHY NOE	HOLY ONE
9. BLAM FO DOG	LAMB OF GOD
10. CINERP FO FILE	PRINCE OF LIFE
11. NOS FO VIDDA	SON OF DAVID
12. DROW FO LEIF	WORD OF LIFE
13. STIRCH	CHRIST
14. HET YAW	THE WAY
15. DORL FO LAL	LORD OF ALL
16. VARIOS	SAVIOR
17. GINK FO SKING	KING OF KINGS
18. DAEH FO ETH CRUCHH	HEAD OF THE CHURCH
*19. LAMINUME	IMMANUEL
*20. FICEH TONESRERONC	CHIEF CORNERSTONE
*21. FUNORWEDL RUNSELCOO	WONDERFUL COUNSELOR
*22. STROUGEHI GEJUD	RIGHTEOUS JUDGE
*23. SRIRERTNOCEU	RESURRECTION
*24. PALAH DAN GAMEO	ALPHA AND OMEGA
*25. LIVERDEER	DELIVERER

Thoughts for the Day

The leader should summarize the ideas presented in the following thoughts.

Jesus felt no resentment, no anger, no desire for punishment for the men who crucified Him. He wanted them to have a second chance. We, too, should allow those who hurt us physically and verbally to receive a second chance. Let's forgive as He forgave.

Memory Verse

A copy of the memory verse should be made for each student to take home. After the leader distributes the copies, the class can say the verse.

"'Father, forgive them, for they do not know what they are doing'" (Luke 23:34).

Prayer

To conclude the session, the leader leads in prayer, allowing time for individual prayers by the students.

Dear God, teach us to forgive as Jesus forgave those who mistreated Him. In Jesus' name, amen.

Next Week

The leader briefly mentions the next week's lesson, "Mary Magdalene Receives a Surprise" (John 20:1-18). Next week we will study about the victory of Jesus over death.

LESSON 24

Mary Magdalene Receives a Surprise

Scripture Text

John 20:1-18

Teacher's Tidbits

The leader should read this section at home before the day of the lesson.

The custom in ancient Palestine was to visit the tomb of a loved one for three days after the body was buried. The Jews believed that the spirit of the dead person hovered over the grave for three days, then it departed because the body became unrecognizable.

Jesus' friends did not come to the tomb on the Sabbath, which was Saturday, because making the journey broke the law. Mary Magdalene loved Jesus so much that she was the first to arrive at the tomb early Sunday morning. Mary went on believing and loving even when she could not understand. Later that morning, she received the glory of being the first to see the risen Christ. Jesus wanted Mary to know that their old relationship of teacher and disciple had changed. The new relationship was mediated by the Holy Spirit whose coming depended on the completion of Jesus' journey to the Father.

John was probably younger and could run faster, so he arrived at the tomb first. But he only peeked in. Peter impulsively went into the tomb. The grave clothes were lying there as if Jesus had evaporated out of them. When John saw the grave clothes, he realized that the Lord had risen from the dead. He was the only one to believe in the resurrection before he saw Jesus alive again.

The resurrection creates a new relationship between Jesus and those who believe in Him—a relationship of knowing Him, not just knowing about Him.

What to Bring

Bibles, pencils, paper, and a curtain for Activity 2.

Questions for Discussion

There may be more than one correct answer for each of the following questions. The leader will ask the questions and wait for the students to provide the answers. The leader should not supply an answer unless it is necessary.

1. Do you know why no one went to the tomb on Saturday? (*They were forbidden by law to travel that distance on the Sabbath.*)

2. What do you know about Mary Magdalene's past? (*Jesus had cast seven demons out of Mary; she witnessed the crucifixion.*)

3. Why did Mary go to the tomb early Sunday morning? (*The Jewish custom was to visit the tomb of a loved one for three days after he was buried; she loved Jesus and she missed Him.*)

4. What did Mary probably think when she saw that the stone had been removed? (*The Jews had taken Jesus' body, or grave robbers had stolen it.*)

5. Why did she locate Simon Peter? (*He was the leader of the disciples; she thought he would know what to do.*)

6. What did she say to Peter and John? (*"They have taken the Lord out of the tomb, and we don't know where they have put Him."*)

7. Which disciple reached the tomb first and what did he do? (*John stopped outside the entrance and peeked in.*)

*8. Would you have been hesitant to walk into the cave if you were John? Explain. (*Allow time for several students to state their opinions on this subject.*)

9. What characteristics do you remember about Peter from past lessons? (*He was impulsive, bold, daring. When he made a mistake, he was not afraid to try again, and difficulties strengthened his faith.*)

10. What did Peter do and see when he reached the tomb? (*He went in and saw the grave clothes lying there as if Jesus had evaporated out of them.*)

11. How does this differ from Lazarus being raised from the dead? (*Lazarus came out with his grave clothes wrapped around him, and eventually he died a natural death on earth again.*)

12. How did John react when he finally entered the tomb? (*He realized that Jesus had risen. He was the only one to believe in the resurrection before seeing Jesus alive again.*)

13. What did Mary see when she bent over to look into the tomb? (*Two angels in white seated where Jesus' body had been.*)

14. Why do you think Mary had trouble recognizing Jesus? (*She did not expect to see Him there; she was crying and probably did not look closely at the person talking to her.*)

15. What did Jesus do so Mary would recognize Him? (*He said her name.*)

*16. When someone calls you by name, are you more likely to recognize the voice? Explain. (*Allow time for several to discuss this.*)

17. Why did Jesus tell her not to hold onto Him? (*Because she needed to let go of their old relationship of teacher and disciple. After He returned to the Father, she could not physically hold onto Him anymore. A new relationship, mediated by the Holy Spirit, resulted from the resurrection.*)

18. What did Jesus tell Mary Magdalene to do? (*To find the disciples and tell them that He was returning to His Father.*)

*19. What does the resurrection of Christ mean to you? (*Allow time for several students to share their views. Because He carried our sins on the cross, died, conquered death, and rose again from the dead, we can have eternal life with Him in Heaven. Now we can know Him as well as know about Him.*)

*20. Challenge: Find one person this week who you can tell about Jesus so that individual can know Him personally.

Activity 1: Endless Word

Have the group form a circle. The first person says a word and then counts 1-2-3-4-5 at a moderate speed. Before this student says five, the youth to the first person's right has to say another word that begins with the last letter of the word just said. This continues around the circle.

It counts as a miss if the person can not think of a word and say it before the person next to him says five. Two misses and the student is out of the game. If it is the individual's first miss, he starts again with any word. No one is allowed to repeat a word.

Activity 2: Who's Behind the Curtain?

Set up a curtain or a sheet for a student to hide behind. The individual who is "it" leaves the room. Another student hides behind the curtain. The person who is "it" comes back into the room. He has five minutes of asking questions to try to find out who is behind the curtain. The game continues with different students as time allows.

Thoughts for the Day

The leader should summarize the ideas presented in the following thoughts.

Peter impulsively ran into the tomb and saw the grave clothes lying there as if Jesus had evaporated out of them. When John entered the tomb, he understood that Jesus had risen from the dead, and he believed Christ had conquered death.

Mary Magdalene went on believing and loving even when she could not understand. She received the glory of being the first to see the risen Christ, and she recognized Him when He said her name.

The resurrection creates a new relationship between Jesus and those who believe in Him. This relationship means knowing Him, not just knowing about Him.

Memory Verse

A copy of the memory verse should be made for each student to take home. After the leader distributes the copies, the class can say the verse aloud together.

"Jesus answered, 'I am the way and the truth and the life. No one comes to the Father except through me'" (John 14:6).

Prayer

To conclude the session, the leader leads in prayer, allowing time for individual prayers by the students.

Dear God, thank You for the gift of Your Son who died on the cross for our sins and conquered death. Teach us to make the most of this new relationship of knowing Jesus. In Jesus' name, amen.

Next Week

The leader briefly mentions the next week's lesson, "Jesus Reveals His Identity in Emmaus" (Luke 24:13-35). What did Christ teach the two Emmaus disciples? When did He reveal His identity to them? Next week we will study about Jesus' surprise visit with two little-known followers of Christ.

Jesus Reveals His Identity in Emmaus

Scripture Text

Luke 24:13-35

Teacher's Tidbits

The leader should read this section at home before the day of the lesson.

The Sunday morning after the crucifixion, two followers of Christ returned from the Passover celebration in Jerusalem to their home in Emmaus, seven miles away. The conversation of the men expressed the violent struggle between hope and fear that raged in their hearts. They mentioned the empty tomb, but they did not understand the meaning of it. This gives us a clear picture of what went on in the hearts of the other disciples on that day.

Jesus mildly rebuked them and went on to explain the Old Testament Scriptures, emphasizing the sufferings of the Messiah. With burning hearts, they listened to His incomparable exposition of the deepest contents of the Old Testament. Jesus waited for their invitation to stay in Emmaus. He did not force Himself upon them. God gave us the greatest and most perilous gift in the world, the gift of free-will. We can use it to invite Christ into our lives or to allow Him to pass by.

During an ordinary meal in an ordinary house, when an ordinary loaf of bread was divided, these men recognized Jesus. This was not the Lord's Supper. It was unusual that Jesus would break the bread since the host normally had that honor.

The realization that Jesus Christ had risen and He lives as the promised Redeemer brought light and joy to their hearts. The men wanted to share their exciting news, so they returned to Jerusalem that same evening.

Today, it is not only at the communion table that we can be with Christ. We can be with Him at the dinner table, too. He is the guest in every home, as well as the host in His Church. We can find Christ everywhere if we will only look for Him.

What to Bring

Bibles, pencils, paper, a whistle, and a dictionary.

Questions for Discussion

There may be more than one correct answer for each of the following questions. The leader will ask the questions and wait for the students to provide the answers. The leader should not supply an answer unless it is necessary.

1. Where was the village of Emmaus? (*Seven miles from Jerusalem.*)

2. Who were these two men? (*Little-known followers of Christ, one was named Cleopas.*)

3. Why would you expect them to stay in Jerusalem another day? (*Jesus told them He would rise from the dead on the third day, but they did not wait in Jerusalem to see even after hearing reports that Jesus was alive.*)

4. What did Jesus ask them? (*"What are you discussing together as you walk along?"*)

5. Why do you think they did not recognize Jesus? (*Allow time for several to give opinions. The sun was in their eyes, Jesus kept them from recognizing Him.*)

6. How did they describe Jesus? (*As a prophet, powerful in word and deed, who they hoped would redeem Israel.*)

*7. If you had been there, how would you have reacted to the news that Jesus' body was not in the tomb and that angels said He was alive? (*Allow time for several students to speculate on this topic. Perhaps remember His words that He would rise again in three days, wonder if He did conquer death.*)

8. How did they react to Mary's news that His body was not in the tomb and He was alive? (*They did not seem excited at all; they did not understand the meaning of the empty tomb.*)

9. How do you see a struggle between hope and fear in the men's words? (*They stood still, their faces downcast. The crucifixion had crushed their hopes.*)

10. How did Jesus respond to their unbelief? (*He mildly rebuked them and explained the Old Testament Scriptures, emphasizing the sufferings of the Messiah.*)

11. When they reached the village, why did Jesus act as if He were going farther? (*Jesus waited for their* invitation to come in; He did not force Himself upon them.)

12. What did the men say to Jesus? (*Stay with us, for the day is almost over.*)

13. If they had not invited Him to stay, would they have learned who He was? (*Probably not at that time.*)

*****14.** Does Jesus wait for an invitation to come into our lives? Explain. (*Yes, He does not force Himself upon us either. We must choose to invite Him into our lives; we must choose to talk to Him regularly in prayer.*)

*****15.** What is the gift of freedom of choice that God has given us? (*We can invite Christ into our lives or allow Him to pass on by; it is the greatest and most perilous gift.*)

16. Was this a communion meal? Explain. (*No, this was an ordinary dinner in an average home.*)

17. How did Jesus use this opportunity of giving thanks and breaking the bread? (*He revealed who He was to them, and then He disappeared.*)

18. How do you think they recognized Jesus? (*He opened their eyes, perhaps they saw the nail prints, or they recognized His manner of breaking bread.*)

19. Why did Jesus appear to these two men from Emmaus? (*So they could realize that He was the Messiah, and so they would go back to Jerusalem and tell the other disciples.*)

*****20.** Challenge: This coming week, find Jesus in one ordinary, every day occurrence in your life.

Activity 1: Add-a-Letter

This game works best with a group of fifteen or less. Have the group sit in a circle. One person begins to spell a word by saying a letter. The next person adds a letter. Each person attempts to add another letter without completing a word. A student gets a point against him if he makes a word by adding his letter. When an individual gets five points, he is out of the game. The winner is the last person left in the game. Words and sequences of letters can be checked in a dictionary.

Activity 2: Clump Tag

This game should be played in a space that has boundaries such as a large room or a basketball court. The game begins with everyone standing around, including the person who is "it." The leader blows the whistle a number of times to signal the start of the game. If the leader blows the whistle three times, the students try to form groups of three. Anyone who is in a group of three cannot be tagged by "it." "It" has a minute to tag as many people as he can.

When the whistle is blown again, everyone is safe,

and they start standing around again. The leader varies the number of times he blows the whistle each time, so the players will not know in advance how big to make their clump. Each time the whistle is blown a series of times in succession, the players form groups the size of the number of whistle toots and lock arms to be safe from "it." The ones who are tagged must leave the game. The winners are the students left after a certain time limit.

Thoughts for the Day

The leader should summarize the ideas presented in the following thoughts.

Jesus appeared to two seemingly insignificant men on the road to Emmaus and explained the deepest contents of the Old Testament Scriptures to them. Because they invited Him to spend the evening, He revealed His true identity to them. They rushed back to Jerusalem to share the news with the other disciples. The men discovered who Jesus was during an ordinary dinner at an average home. We, too, can be with Christ and discover who He is at our dinner table and during the everyday events of our lives.

Memory Verse

A copy of the memory verse should be made for each student to take home. After the leader distributes the copies, the class can say the verse aloud together.

"'For I was hungry and you gave me something to eat, I was thirsty and you gave me something to drink, I was a stranger and you invited me in'" (Matthew 25:35).

Prayer

To conclude the session, the leader leads in prayer, allowing time for individual prayers by the students.

Dear Lord, thank You for revealing Your true identity to Your followers in Biblical times and to us today. In Jesus' name, amen.

Next Week

The leader briefly mentions the next week's lesson, "Jesus Appears to His Disciples" (John 20:19-31). Next week we will study about a message Jesus brought to His disciples to prepare them for their ministries.

Jesus Appears to His Disciples

Scripture Text

John 20:19-31

Teacher's Tidbits

The leader should read this section at home before the day of the lesson.

After the crucifixion, the disciples probably continued to meet in the upper room where the Last Supper was held. They were aware of the bitterness of the Jews, so they met in secret, fearfully listening to every footstep and every knock on their door.

Suddenly, Jesus stood there with them. He breathed on His disciples and gave them the Holy Spirit. However, they were to wait until the day of Pentecost to begin their ministry. Through the disciples, Jesus ultimately created the Church.

Jesus Christ needs the Church. His message could never be taken to everyone unless the Church carried it. The Church needs Jesus. It needs a power and an authority to back its message. Each Christian needs someone to turn to when facing doubt and difficulty. The Church can proclaim the forgiveness of sins to all. Jesus promised that when two or three gather in His name, He is there with them.

Thomas made the mistake of withdrawing from the fellowship of the disciples to face his sorrow alone. Because he was not present in the upper room, he missed Jesus' first visit. We often shut ourselves away when sadness overwhelms us. Yet, this is the time when we should seek the fellowship of Christ's people, for it is there that we are likely to meet Him face-to-face.

What to Bring

Bibles, pencils, paper sacks for all the students, a ball of heavy yarn, and scissors.

Questions for Discussion

There may be more than one correct answer for each of the following questions. The leader will ask the questions and wait for the students to provide the answers. The leader should not supply an answer unless it is necessary.

1. Do you know where the disciples met? (*Probably in the upper room where they celebrated the Passover with Jesus.*)

2. Why did they lock the doors? (*They were afraid that the angry, Jewish officials would come after them next and crucify them.*)

3. Why did Jesus show the disciples His hands and His side? (*He wanted to make sure they believed that He stood before them, that their faith was strong enough for the mission of starting His Church.*)

4. What did He mean when He said, "'As the Father has sent me, I am sending you'"? (*They were the beginning of the Church that would carry His message of salvation around the world.*)

5. What gift did Jesus give His disciples to equip them for their ministry? (*The Holy Spirit, but their ministry did not start until after Pentecost.*)

*6. Who is the Holy Spirit? (*The third person of the Trinity, the Holy Spirit was sent to live and work in the disciples and in Christians today.*)

*7. Have you felt the Holy Spirit working inside of you? (*Do not force anyone to answer this highly personal question, but everyone should think about it.*)

8. Why do you think Thomas was not with the disciples when Jesus first appeared? (*He withdrew from the others and experienced his sorrow alone.*)

9. What did Thomas miss by not being in the upper room? (*He missed the first appearance of Jesus to His disciples.*)

*10. Have you ever shut yourself away alone when you felt sad and upset? (*Allow time for a few who are willing to share their experiences.*)

*11. What might be a better way to handle our emotions when we are terribly upset? (*To talk to a friend, pastor, or relative about what is bothering us.*)

12. How would you describe Thomas' personality? (*He doubted; he was loyal but skeptical; yet he was the one who offered to go to Jerusalem to die with Jesus.*)

13. What kind of proof of Christ's resurrection did he ask for? (*He wanted to put his fingers where the nails were and place his hand in Jesus' side.*)

14. Why did Jesus allow Thomas to participate in this experiment? (*Jesus knew that once Thomas stopped*

doubting and believed, he would go the ultimate limit to carry the Church around the world. Thomas is credited with taking the Gospel to India.)

15. What did Thomas say to Jesus? (*"My Lord and my God."*)

16. How did Jesus respond? (*"Because you have seen me you have believed; blessed are those who have not seen and yet have believed."*)

*17. Who are those who have not seen and yet believe? (*Christians who never met Jesus. Christians, like us today, who accept Jesus and believe in Him through faith.*)

*18. Why does Jesus need the Church? (*The message of Jesus Christ can only be taken to those who have never heard of Him by people who believe in Him, those who form His Church.*)

*19. What is meant by the Church? (*All the people around the world who have accepted Jesus Christ as their Savior.*)

*20. Challenge: Find one way to take the message of Jesus Christ to someone who does not know who He is.

Activity 1: Sack Sign-up

Since this is the last lesson, it may represent the last time together for many of the students. Here is an activity that will give each one of them something to remember the others by.

Give each student a pen or pencil and a small paper sack to place over the right hand if right-handed and the left hand if left-handed. Everyone goes around the room getting signatures on their sacks. Remind them that they must not write with their usual writing hand. The first person to obtain signatures from everyone in the room is the winner. They may take their sacks home as a memory of those who were in the class.

Activity 2: Yarn Circle

This activity is most effective if done at the end of class. The group should be seated in a circle. Each person is given a piece of yarn about eighteen inches long to represent individuality. Go around the circle having each student share one thing learned in this series of classes. After speaking, the youth ties his yarn to the person sitting next to him. After everyone has spoken, the yarn will form a circle representing the unity of the group and the fact that we are all one in Christ.

The group may then want to pray and reflect on Christ, the cross, and the resurrection. If allowed, the Lord's Supper may be served. To close, the leader goes to each person and cuts a section off the yarn, leaving one knot on each individual's section. The piece of yarn that the young person receives represents the fact that we are all individuals, but the knot reminds them that we all belong to the Church of Christ and are connected to others in the group.

Thoughts for the Day

The leader should summarize the ideas presented in the following thoughts.

After Jesus was crucified on the cross, the disciples met in the upper room, afraid the Jews would come after them next. Jesus brought the Holy Spirit to His disciples and convinced them of His resurrection. He filled them with peace, confidence, and a desire to carry the Gospel to all nations whatever the cost.

The Church is more than buildings and denominations. The Church is people who have accepted Christ as their personal Savior. We all have been given the gift of the Holy Spirit who works through us to bring others to Christ.

Memory Verse

A copy of the memory verse should be made for each student to take home. After the leader distributes the copies, the class can say the verse aloud together.

"Then Jesus told him, 'Because you have seen me, you have believed; blessed are those who have not seen and yet have believed'" (John 20:29).

Prayer

To conclude the session, the teacher leads in prayer, allowing time for individual prayers by the students.

Dear God, thank You for giving us the gift of the Holy Spirit. Teach us to bring the Gospel to others who do not know You; for You live in us. In Jesus' name, amen.